World War II: The War in Europe

by John J. Vail

America's
WARS

Lucent Books, P.O. Box 289011, San Diego, CA 92198-0011

Books in the America's Wars Series

The Revolutionary War
The Indian Wars
The War of 1812
The Mexican-American War
The Civil War
The Spanish-American War

World War I
World War II: The War in the Pacific
World War II: The War in Europe
The Korean War
The Vietnam War
The Persian Gulf War

Library of Congress Cataloging-in-Publication Data

Vail, John J.
   World War II: the war in Europe/by John J. Vail.
      p.   cm.—(America's wars)
   Includes bibliographical references and index.
   Summary: Discusses the notable events of World War II that took
place in Europe, from the ominous chain of events leading up to
Germany's invasion of Poland to the death of Hitler.
   ISBN 1–56006–407–2
   1. World War, 1939–1945—Juvenile literature. [1. World War,
1939–1945.] I. Title. II. Title: World War 2. 2. III. Title: World
War two. IV. Series.
D743.7.V35 1991
940.53—dc20   91–23062

Contents

Foreword

War, justifiable or not, is a descent into madness. George Washington, America's first president and commander-in-chief of its armed forces, wrote that his most fervent wish was "to see this plague of mankind, war, banished from the earth." Most, if not all of the forty presidents who succeeded Washington have echoed similar sentiments. Despite this, not one generation of Americans since the founding of the republic has been spared the maelstrom of war. In its brief history of just over two hundred years, the United States has been a combatant in eleven major wars. And four of those conflicts have occurred in the last fifty years.

America's reasons for going to war have differed little from those of most nations. Political, social, and economic forces were at work which either singly or in combination ushered America into each of its wars. A desire for independence motivated the Revolutionary War. The fear of annihilation led to the War of 1812. A related fear, that of having the nation divided, precipitated the Civil War. The need to contain an aggressor nation brought the United States into the Korean War. And territorial ambition lay behind the Mexican-American and the Indian Wars. Like all countries, America, at different times in its history, has been victimized by these forces and its citizens have been called to arms.

Whatever reasons may have been given to justify the use of military force, not all of America's wars have been popular. From the Revolutionary War to the Vietnam War, support of the people has alternately waxed and waned. For example, less than half of the colonists backed America's war of independence. In fact, most historians agree that at least one-third were committed to maintaining America's colonial status. During the Spanish-American War, a strong antiwar movement also developed. Resistance to the war was so high that the Democratic party made condemning the war a significant part of its platform in an attempt to lure voters into voting Democratic. The platform stated that "the burning issue of imperialism growing out of the Spanish war involves the very existence of the Republic and the destruction of our free institutions." More recently, the Vietnam War divided the nation like no other conflict had since the Civil War. The mushrooming antiwar movements in most major cities and colleges throughout the United States did more to bring that war to a conclusion than did actions on the battlefield.

Yet, there have been wars which have enjoyed overwhelming public support. World Wars I and II were popular because people believed that the survival of America's democratic institutions was at stake. In both wars, the American people rallied with an enthusiasm and spirit of self-sacrifice that was remarkable for a country with such a diverse population. Support for food and fuel rationing, the purchase of war bonds, a high rate of voluntary enlistments, and countless other forms of voluntarism, were characteristic of the people's response to those wars. Most recently, the Persian Gulf War prompted an unprecedented show of support even though the United States was not directly threatened by the conflict. Rallies in support of U.S. troops were widespread. Tens of thousands of individuals, including families, friends, and well-wishers of the troops sent packages of food, cosmetics, clothes, cassettes, and suntan oil. And even more supporters wrote letters to unknown soldiers that were forwarded to the military front. In fact, most public opinion polls revealed that up to 90 percent of all Americans approved of their nation's involvement.

The complex interplay of events and purposes that leads to military conflict should be included in a history of any war. A simple chronicling of battles and casualty lists at best offers only a partial history of war. Wars do not spontaneously erupt; nor does their memory perish. They are driven by underlying causes, fueled by policymakers, fought and supported by citizens, and remembered by those plotting a nation's future. For these reasons wars, or the fear of wars, will always leave an indelible stamp on any nation's history and influence its future.

The purpose of this series is to provide a full understanding of America's Wars by presenting each war in a historical context. Each of the twelve volumes focuses on the events that led up to the war, the war itself, its impact on the home front, and its aftermath and influence upon future conflicts. The unique personalities, the dramatic acts of courage and compassion, as well as the despair and horror of war are all presented in this series. Together, they show why America's wars have dominated American consciousness in the past as well as how they guide many political decisions of today. In these vivid and objective accounts, students will gain an understanding of why America became involved in these conflicts, and how historians, military and government officials, and others have come to understand and interpret that involvement.

Chronology of Events

June 28, 1919
Treaty of Versailles signed by Allies and Germany.

March 1936
Nazi Germany moves troops into the Rhineland.

March 1938
German troops invade Austria; union of Germany and Austria proclaimed.

September 1938
Munich conference. Area of Czechoslovakia given to Germany.

November 9, 1938
Kristallnacht; Nazis rampage against German Jews.

August 23, 1939
Nonaggression pact signed between the Soviet Union and Germany.

September 1, 1939
German troops invade Poland. World War II begins.

May 10, 1940
German troops invade the Netherlands, Belgium, and France. Winston Churchill becomes British prime minister.

May 26–June 4, 1940
Evacuation of Allied troops from Dunkerque.

June 22, 1940
France signs armistice with Germany.

August 13, 1940
Battle of Britain begins.

June 22, 1941
Operation Barbarossa begins; German invasion of the Soviet Union.

December 7, 1941
Japanese attack on Pearl Harbor; the United States enters the war.

October 23, 1942
Battle of Alamein begins.

November 8, 1942
American and British troops land in Morocco and Algeria.

January 31, 1943
German Sixth Army surrenders at Battle of Stalingrad.

May 13, 1943
German troops in North Africa surrender.

September 9, 1943
Allied landings in Salerno, Italy.

June 4, 1944
American troops enter Rome.

June 6, 1944
D day; Allies invade Normandy.

August 25, 1944
Paris liberated by the Allies.

December 16, 1944
Germany's last military offensive; Battle of the Bulge begins.

March 7, 1945
American army crosses the Rhine.

April 12, 1945
Roosevelt dies; Harry Truman becomes American president.

April 25, 1945
American and Red Army troops make contact at Torgau along the Elbe River; Berlin surrounded by Soviet army.

April 30, 1945
Hitler commits suicide.

May 7, 1945
Unconditional surrender of all German forces to the Allies.

May 8, 1945
Victory in Europe Day.

August 6, 1945
First atomic bomb dropped on Hiroshima, Japan.

August 9, 1945
Second atomic bomb dropped on Nagasaki, Japan.

August 14, 1945
Japan surrenders; World War II ends.

INTRODUCTION

"The War to End All Wars"

World War II was a vast endeavor. For many of the nations involved in it, the war remains a vivid, excruciating memory. In Europe, the war destroyed whole cities and left millions homeless. For the Jewish population, the war was particularly crippling. Hitler's extermination campaign killed over six million Jews from all over Europe. After the war, thousands of others relocated, unable to forget the horror they had experienced in Europe.

Beneath the vast devastation of the Second World War, there remained the story of the people who fought it. Every key battle of the war, no matter the tactical genius of the commanders or the incredibly sophisticated weapons of the armies, came down to simple acts of bravery and courage by individual soldiers. In any chronicle of a war, the grand strategy of generals and heads of state should also be coupled with a vivid, realistic portrait of the fighting which the average soldier experienced. *World War II: The War in Europe* attempts to synthesize these events. In it are the furious dogfights over the skies of London during the Battle of Britain; the brutal hand-to-hand combat in the snowy streets of Stalingrad; the grueling fighting in the mountainsides of Italy; the bloody struggles on the beaches and hedgerows of Normandy. It is the story of the quiet courage and dignity of the American soldier in the face of constant physical discomfort, bone-deep weariness and grave danger.

World War II created the world in which we live. It reshaped the entire geography of Europe and paved the way for a new system of international politics. Although the United States was left untouched by the horrible devastation which the war inflicted on Europe, American society was nevertheless profoundly affected by the war. It transformed the United States into the most powerful military and economic nation on earth. It brought unparalleled prosperity to millions of Americans. It changed Americans' living patterns and marked an important step in the transformation of race relations. In short, World War II was perhaps the single most important event in twentieth-century American history.

The Second World War was also the only conflict in the century that the American people overwhelmingly supported. Americans saw the war as a crusade between good and evil. They believed, without reservation, that the war was absolutely necessary to preserve human decency and democracy in the world. It is for this reason that World War II has come to be viewed in American history as the last of the "good wars."

CHAPTER ONE

A World at War

World War II was one of the largest events in human history. From 1939 to 1945, more than sixty million soldiers from forty countries were involved in the conflict. It was fought across six of the world's continents and all of its oceans. Fifty million people were killed. Hundreds of millions were wounded. Countless homes were destroyed, and the countryside and cities of Europe and Asia were ravaged.

World War II was the first time that the United States had ever fought on such a vast scale. Sixteen million Americans were mobilized into the country's armed forces. American soldiers fought courageously in North Africa, Italy, France, Germany, and

The devastation of war is evident in this 1945 photograph taken of the banks of the Pegnitz River in the German city of Nuremberg. Nuremberg was one of many cities destroyed in the war.

Medics remove a casualty from the battlefield near Brest, France, one of millions of casualties of the war.

An American soldier tends to the wounds of a young Nazi injured in the fighting.

in the Pacific. American armies played a decisive role in winning the war. The Second World War also had a profound effect on American society. It transformed the United States into the most powerful military and economic nation on earth. It brought unparalleled prosperity to millions of Americans. World War II was perhaps the single most important event in twentieth-century American history.

Why did World War II begin? How can its origins be explained? An answer to these questions must begin by examining the larger historical events that paved the way for the conflict. In this regard, three episodes in the early twentieth century were critical: the Russian Revolution of 1917, the Great Depression from 1929 to 1933, and above all, World War I from 1914 to 1918. "The First [World] War explains the Second, in fact caused it, insofar as one event explains another," wrote A. J. P. Taylor in *The Origins of the Second World War.* "The link between the two wars went deeper. Germany fought specifically in the Second War to reverse the verdict of the First and to destroy the settlement that followed it."

An entire generation of European youths lost their lives in the senseless slaughter of World War I. That war was so horribly destructive that the victorious Allies, led by Great Britain, France, and the United States, were united in their desire to prevent another such conflict from ever occurring again. Their common goal was to ensure that World War I became "the war to end all wars." In 1919, at the end of World War I, an international organization of many of the world's countries, called the League of Nations, was established to promote world peace and security. The organization called for the abolition of secret treaties between nations, mutual respect for international boundaries, and general disarmament. Yet the goals of the League of Nations remained unfulfilled. Because its members rejected the idea of maintaining an international military force, the organization could not enforce its policies. This would have a dramatic impact on the outbreak of the next war.

After their victory, the Allies also wanted to reduce Germany's capability of waging war. To the Allies, Germany was the aggressor and was responsible for the terrible destruction wreaked by World War I. The terms of the Versailles Treaty of 1919 left Germany militarily and politically powerless. The treaty limited Germany to a standing army of only 100,000 men and eliminated its air force, artillery, and submarines. No troops, artillery, or bases could be placed in the Rhineland area on Germany's western border. This was supposed to make it less easy for Germany to invade France and to ensure that any future war between France and Germany would be fought on German soil. The German government was forced to pay the Allies several hundred million dollars for losses and damages suffered during the war. The productive German provinces of Alsace-Lorraine and Sudetenland were given to France and Czechoslovakia respectively. Poland also received territory from Germany, including the "Polish corridor." This was a narrow strip of land that cut off East Prussia from the rest of Germany and extended to the Baltic Sea near Danzig, in Poland.

Germans Resent the Treaty's Terms

The Versailles Treaty provoked tremendous resentment among all Germans. They felt the provisions of the treaty were unfair and made a mockery of the "just peace" that the Allies had promised. Nevertheless, the leaders of Germany's new democratic government, known as the Weimar Republic, felt they had no choice but to approve the treaty. They were convinced that if they refused, Allied troops would occupy Germany and collapse the German economy. German politicians denounced their government for accepting the treaty. These politicians believed the government had betrayed the German people.

In the decade following the Versailles Treaty, various political groups challenged the democratic German government. Right-wing groups and paramilitary organizations appeared throughout the country. The Bolshevik Revolution of 1917, which established a communist government in Russia, inspired several similar but unsuccessful revolutionary uprisings in Germany. The German middle classes feared that Russia's revolution would spread to their country. But, the greatest danger to German democracy would not come from the communists.

On November 8, 1923, a tiny group called the Nazi party attempted to overthrow the democratic German government. Led by Adolf Hitler, a group of Nazis surrounded a beer hall in Munich where a political meeting was taking place. The Nazis took government officials hostage, and Hitler proclaimed the

Adolf Hitler

Adolf Hitler was born in April 1889, in a small Austrian town near the Bavarian border. He quit high school at age sixteen and lived the next three years in Linz. Hitler did not take a regular job but instead spent his time daydreaming, visiting the opera, and painting. Hitler dreamed of becoming a great artist, but he flunked the entrance examination at the Vienna Academy of Fine Arts. From 1909 to 1913, he lived in Vienna as a vagabond, working odd jobs and selling hand-painted postcards on the city streets. Hitler called it "the saddest period of my life."

With no other prospects, Hitler joined the German infantry at the start of World War I. He became a corporal and was wounded in 1916. He received Germany's highest military honor, the Iron Cross, First Class, for bravery in battle. This was a rare achievement for an enlisted soldier. Germany's defeat profoundly affected Hitler's life. It gave him a permanent hatred of democratic politics and a strong belief in himself.

After the war, Hitler decided to enter politics. He was twenty-nine years old with no profession, no education, and no friends. In 1921, he joined a small political party, the National Socialist Workers party, or Nazis. Hitler suddenly revealed a ferocious energy and drive. He proved to be a brilliant organizer, propagandist, and orator. Hitler became their leader within a year and chose the swastika, an ancient Hindu sign, as the Nazi symbol.

Hitler's rise to power was made possible by a combination of terror tactics and skillful propaganda. His political opponents were beaten and their meetings disrupted by Nazi storm troopers. The Nazis staged torch-lit rallies organized by their minister of propaganda, Joseph Goebbels. At huge party rallies, the crowd often stood hypnotized by Hitler's mesmerizing speeches. The chant of "Heil Hitler, Heil Hitler" (Hail Hitler) would echo through the stadium. Men threw their arms out in the Nazi salute and continued the chorus, "Sieg Heil, Sieg Heil" (Hail victory). Once in power, Hitler established a brutal, terrifying dictatorship. After his humiliating defeat at the end of World War II, he committed suicide on April 30, 1945.

Adolf Hitler (right) rose to power by using terror and propaganda. He inspired a near-hypnotic allegiance in Germany's young people (left).

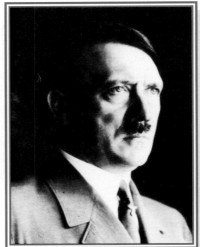

formation of a new government. The Nazi uprising was quickly squashed, and Hitler was sentenced to five years in prison for his role in the so-called "beer hall putsch." Although the attempted overthrow failed, it transformed Hitler into a national figure. In just over a decade, his popularity would increase so much that he would become dictator of Germany.

While in prison, Hitler wrote his autobiography, *Mein Kampf* (My Struggle). The book was a revealing portrait of Hitler's political beliefs and personality. Hitler believed German democracy should be overthrown and a dictatorship put in its place. He believed Germany required a fuhrer, or leader, whose absolute authority would be unchallenged. Hitler envisioned a German empire that would rule the European continent for one thousand years. He was certain that God had chosen the German people to be the master race, and he believed it was his destiny to lead them to world power.

The German conquest of Europe, he wrote, could be achieved only by war. Hitler glorified the idea of war and promised to regain Germany's self-esteem after its humiliating defeat in World War I. Hitler vowed to destroy France and Britain. He also wanted to conquer the Soviet Union to provide more space for the German people and to ensure the destruction of communism. In his book, Hitler also revealed a fanatic hatred of the Jewish people. He considered Jews to be an "inferior race" and blamed them for all of Germany's troubles. Hitler promised that in the future, only "pure Aryans"—non-Jewish, Nordic whites—would be allowed to be part of the German nation. Most people who read *Mein Kampf* did not take it seriously. Once Hitler came to power, however, it became an accurate blueprint of his policies.

After his release from jail, Hitler said he would not attempt another violent overthrow of the German government. Instead, he tried to make the Nazi party more powerful and influential. In the 1928 elections, the Nazis had 100,000 members, but they received only 800,000 votes out of the 31 million cast. After the Great Depression of 1929, however, the Nazis did become a powerful force in German politics. The stock market crash in New York on October 29, 1929, spread to Germany, where the effect on the country's economy was devastating. Unemployment rose from 1.3 million in 1929 to 6 million in 1932. The German middle classes' life savings were wiped out.

Hitler and his Nazi party hold a rally in Nuremberg in 1928.

Adolf Hitler and the Nazis Rise to Power

The Nazis thrived in these troubled times. The German people looked for easy explanations and simple solutions to end their misery. The skillful Nazi propaganda campaign blamed the depression on Germany's democratic leaders and a Jewish

German troops attend mass roll call in 1935 (above); Nazi party members confiscate books and magazines considered dangerous or offensive (top, left); signs begin appearing throughout Germany warning citizens that "The Jews are our Misfortune" (top, right).

conspiracy. Hitler promised to improve the German economy. He told Germans that they would no longer have to make payments to the Allies, that every German would have a job, and that the country would become strong again. The Nazi solutions appealed to the suffering middle classes. Wealthy business people also supported Hitler because he was an anti-communist.

Nazis set out to intimidate their political opponents. The private Nazi army, known as the storm troopers, numbered 300,000 by 1930. They assaulted members of other political parties and disrupted opponents' political meetings. Both Nazi tactics paid off. In 1929, the Nazis received only 3 percent of the electoral vote. A year later, they were the second largest party in the German legislature.

The real breakthrough came in 1932. Hitler ran for president against the eighty-four-year-old former field marshal Paul von Hindenburg. Although Hitler lost by seven million votes, the Nazi party members gained many seats in the parliament. Through his political expertise, Hitler made a secret pact with his rivals to attain power. On January 30, 1933, he was named chancellor of Germany. Hitler agreed to a government cabinet that contained only three Nazi ministers out of eleven. His rivals believed they could control the Nazi leader, but Hitler would not be contented until he became the absolute ruler of Germany.

It took Hitler only a year and a half to realize this goal. On February 27, 1933, the parliament building was destroyed by an arsonist. Although the fire was secretly set by the Nazis, the blame fell on a lone Communist worker. Hitler claimed the German Communist party was organizing a vast conspiracy to overthrow the country. He declared a state of emergency and suspended all civil liberties. In a state of emergency, Hitler had the power to crush his opponents. Months later, the Nazis intimidated the members of the parliament into passing legislation that amended the German constitution to give Hitler total power as chancellor. In 1934, he named himself fuhrer, absolute ruler of Germany.

Hitler's Nazi Dictatorship

In his new role, Hitler completely transformed Germany into a military dictatorship. His personal bodyguards, the SS, became a secret police under Hitler's exclusive control. Independent trade unions were banned. All political opponents were arrested. All political parties except for the Nazis were outlawed. No dissent was tolerated. Books that were considered dangerous or offensive were destroyed in huge book-burning rallies. The Nazis passed laws that denied German Jews the right to vote or to marry non-Jews. The persecution of the Jews reached a climax on November 9, 1938. During *Kristallnacht* (night of broken glass), thousands of Jewish businesses and synagogues were destroyed or burned. Jewish property was confiscated. More than thirty thousand Jews were arrested and sent to prison camps.

At age forty-five, Hitler had already conquered Germany and so set out to conquer all of Europe. His dream of establishing a German empire over the continent could now be realized. Although Hitler believed war would be inevitable to achieve his goal, he had no prepared timetable. Hitler hoped to seize as much territory as possible through bluff and intimidation first. He was convinced that the other European powers had neither the will nor the capacity to stop him.

The leaders of the European democracies observed Hitler's brutal rise to power. But in the years to follow, they would, time after time, fail to understand his unswerving determination to rule Europe. Some would underestimate his ambitions; others thought his efforts could be stopped if necessary. Still others believed that the Soviet Union was the greater threat to international security.

Germans were urged to boycott Jewish businesses. The placard hanging outside this Jewish-owned store in Berlin reads, "Germans, defend yourselves, do not buy from Jews."

Once Hitler had conquered Germany, he set out to conquer all of Europe. Here, he speaks to Nazi party members and troops.

German Pre-War Expansion

All of Europe failed to counter Hitler's aggression. From 1936 to 1939, Hitler made a series of bold moves to increase Germany's power. No one incident was enough to prompt the European countries to act together to resist the Nazis, but together these events laid the groundwork for World War II.

Hitler Violates Versailles Treaty Terms

Hitler's first step was to ignore the Versailles settlement and restore Germany to its former power. He quickly began an ambitious program to rebuild the German tank divisions, or panzer divisions; the German air force (Luftwaffe); and the submarines. In 1936, Hitler sent two German divisions into the Rhineland. This, too, was a blatant violation of the Versailles treaty. This move could have been a dangerous one for Hitler. At the time, the French army was clearly superior to Germany's, and France could have easily made Germany withdraw with just the smallest show of force. This might have stopped Hitler: "A retreat on our part," Hitler admitted, "would have spelled collapse." But, Hitler was gambling that the French would not mobilize their army. His recklessness succeeded. The French wanted peace at almost any price, so they did nothing. This was perhaps the last chance to halt Nazi aggression without risking an all-out war. Instead, Hitler's victory only increased his confidence and spurred him on to even greater acts of aggression.

Hitler's next target was Austria. Hitler remembered how the League of Nations had done nothing to stop the Japanese from occupying Manchuria in 1931 or to halt Italy's conquest of Ethiopia in 1935. Hitler concluded that the League of Nations would not oppose his own aggressive plans. In March 1938, Hitler announced that the chancellor of Austria had asked him to help squelch a rebellion. German troops used this reason to march into Austria. Hitler made a triumphant entry into Vienna and declared Austria to be a part of the German nation. The European democracies denounced Germany's violation of another nation's borders, but they did nothing. Hitler then turned his sights on Czechoslovakia. He demanded that German citizens living in Sudetenland, now part of Czechoslovakia, be allowed to rejoin Germany. Hitler threatened an immediate war unless his demand was met. German and Czechoslovakian troops massed on the border.

This time, however, Prime Minister Neville Chamberlain of Great Britain and Prime Minister Edouard Daladier of France did get involved. Chamberlain believed Hitler could be trusted to act in good faith. After a series of meetings in Munich, the British and French forced the Czech government to accept an agreement to give Germany Sudetenland, almost one-third of Czech territory. Chamberlain believed the agreement would save Europe from war. He told reporters that it guaranteed "peace for our time." The Munich agreement was widely applauded in both Great Britain and France. People in both countries did not want to be involved

Hitler took control of Austria in March 1938. At left, German police march through the Austrian town of Imst. At right, a Czechoslovakian woman salutes the arrival of Hitler's forces and cries.

Division of Powers 1939–1940

SCALE OF MILES
0 100 200 300 400

Germany and Slovakia
Allied Nations
Neutral Nations
German Occupation
Soviet Occupation

NORTH SEA

NORWAY

SWEDEN

FINLAND

ESTONIA

BALTIC SEA

LATVIA

LITHUANIA

Danzig

EAST PRUSSIA

U. S. S. R.

DENMARK

Northern Ireland

UNITED KINGDOM

IRELAND

GREAT BRITAIN

London

ATLANTIC OCEAN

NETHERLANDS

BELGIUM

Dunkerque

LUX.

Paris

Berlin

Warsaw

POLAND

GERMANY

SLOVAKIA

BESSARABIA

Vichy

SWITZ.

AUSTRIA

HUNGARY

FRANCE

ITALY

RUMANIA

Danube R.

PORTUGAL

SPAIN

YUGOSLAVIA

ADRIATIC SEA

BULGARIA

BLACK SEA

MEDITERRANEAN SEA

ALBANIA (Italy)

GREECE

TURKEY

in a war over Czechoslovakia. Yet there were a few voices who warned that appeasing Hitler was foolish and made a future war with Germany inevitable. In the British House of Commons, Winston Churchill, who was a member of Parliament, criticized Chamberlain: "You were given the choice between war and dishonor. You chose dishonor and you will have war."

Hitler, of course, had no intention of honoring the agreement. Within six months, German soldiers invaded the rest of Czechoslovakia. British and French leaders issued public warnings, saying any further attacks would risk war. Hitler still did not believe the Allies had the will to fight. Instead of complying, he promptly demanded that the "Polish corridor" be returned to Germany. Great Britain and France informed the Polish government that they would declare war on Germany if Poland were attacked.

The European powers began to discuss the formation of an alliance against Nazi Germany. The dictator of the Soviet Union, Joseph Stalin, proposed a military treaty between his nation, Britain, and France in which each would pledge to fight Germany should any of the three or their allies be attacked.

Joseph Stalin

Joseph Vissarionovich Dzhugashvili, or Stalin, was born in 1879. He grew up in the province of Georgia, which was then part of the Russian empire. Stalin was the son of a shoemaker. He trained for the priesthood in a seminary in Tbilisi but was expelled in 1899 for "rebellious attitudes."

In 1901, Stalin went "underground" and spent the next sixteen years in the revolutionary movement against the czar, the monarch of Russia. He was a member of the revolutionary Bolshevik party, which promoted the establishment of a communist government in Russia. He adopted the pseudonym of Stalin from the Russian word for "steel." He was repeatedly imprisoned and exiled by the Czarist government for his political activities. After the 1917 Bolshevik Revolution (which transformed Russia into the communist Soviet Union), Stalin became one of the leading members of the new government. He became head of the Communist party after the death of Vladimir Lenin, the first leader of the Soviet Union, in 1924.

During the next decade, Stalin became a ruthless dictator. He expelled his main rival, Leon Trotsky, from the country in 1927 and in 1940 had him murdered in Mexico. During the 1930s, Stalin instituted a reign of terror that completely wiped out all potential opponents and rivals. Peasants were kicked off their land and driven to starvation. A huge system of prison labor camps was established throughout the country for millions of political opponents and innocent victims. It is estimated that as many as fifteen million people may have perished during Stalin's murderous reign.

During his ruthless reign, Joseph Stalin sent millions of political opponents and others to labor camps where many perished.

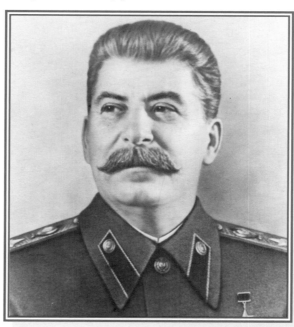

Churchill admitted Stalin had made a "fair offer," but it was rejected by Chamberlain. The major stumbling block was the Polish government, which refused to allow Soviet troops to enter its territory to fight the Germans in case of a war. Without Soviet support, Poland would be quickly overrun if the Germans attacked, and an alliance would be useless. The talks collapsed, and the threat of war grew closer.

Germany and the Soviet Union Form a Shocking Alliance

On August 24, 1939, Nazi Germany and the Soviet Union shocked the entire world. Their foreign ministers signed a ten-year nonaggression pact. This alliance meant that Hitler could attack Poland and western Europe without fear of a Soviet invasion from the east. Since Stalin could not reach an agreement with Europe, he felt he had no choice but to remain neutral. But Hitler had made the treaty very lucrative for the Soviet Union. The Soviet Union was allowed to occupy half of Poland and to take over the Baltic states of Latvia, Estonia, and Lithuania once the war against Poland began. Stalin thought the alliance would give him valuable time to prepare the Soviet forces in case Nazi Germany turned against his own country in the future.

On August 31, 1939, German radio reported that Polish troops had attacked the small southeastern German border town of Gleiwetz. The Polish army had raided a tiny customs post and radio station. But in fact, the entire incident had been staged by Nazi Germany's secret police, the SS. Hitler, in typical fashion, wanted to have a reason to start the war against Poland. SS men, dressed in Polish uniforms, performed the assault. They killed a number of German prison inmates beforehand, then moved the bodies to the small town. There, the bodies were repeatedly shot to provide evidence of a heated battle. German officials gleefully displayed the bullet-strewn bodies to the world press as proof of Poland's treachery. The next morning, September 1, 1939, one million German soldiers crossed the border and invaded Poland. World War II had begun.

Great Britain and France declared war on Germany two days later. When Germany invaded, it left only twenty-five divisions guarding its western borders, where they faced five times as many French soldiers. Hitler was convinced, rightly as it turned out, that France would not attack him from the west. Instead, France simply reinforced its defenses and stood by while the German army took control of Poland. The German invasion was the first full-scale demonstration of the effectiveness of German blitzkrieg tactics. The term blitzkrieg means "lightning war" and refers to the use of forceful and speedy surprise-attack techniques.

German Advances, 1939–1940

Germany invades
Denmark and Norway
April 1940

Germany invades
Low Countries
May 1940

Battle of France
May–June 1940

WWII begins when
Germany invades Poland
September 1, 1939

Legend:
- Germany and Slovakia
- Allied Nations
- Neutral Nations
- German Occupation
- Soviet Occupation
- German Drives

German troops advanced quickly, with concentrated panzer units spearheading the attack. Polish soldiers on horses defended their country against German tanks. The Polish capital, Warsaw, was encircled and subjected to intense bombardment. Although they put up a valiant struggle, the Poles were no match for the better-trained and better-equipped Germans. The war lasted a mere five weeks. Almost one-half million Poles were killed, and 700,000 were taken prisoner. The Germans lost only 11,000 people.

The Fall of France

A strange period of watchfulness and anticipation followed, known as the Phony War. Great Britain, France, and its allies were in a state of war against Germany. Yet for the next nine months, no fighting took place. Instead, both sides began to prepare for war. The Allied armies were slightly larger than the Germans. Except for German superiority in fighter planes, both sides were equally matched in military equipment. But the Germans enjoyed a distinct advantage in strategy, leadership, and fighting spirit.

The key to the French strategy was the Maginot line. This was a series of heavily defended fortifications that ran north from the Swiss border, along the western banks of the Rhine River to southernmost Belgium. These fortifications were in place to protect France's eastern border, and the French military command believed the Maginot line was impregnable. The Germans would then be able to attack only through northern Belgium. This is where the bulk of the French and British armies was concentrated. The French military leaders remembered fighting World War I and envisioned a repetition of the slow-moving battles and drawn-out trench warfare. And this is the kind of war they prepared for. But the German blitzkrieg tactics meant this strategy would be completely ineffective. The swift, concentrated tank and airplane attacks by the Germans would overwhelm the slow-moving French forces.

When deciding where to direct his attack, Hitler, over the objection of his military commanders, proposed a daring plan. He suggested the main German assault, led by massive tank divisions, should be launched through the Ardennes Forest in Belgium. This region lay north of the Maginot line. The Allies believed a large-scale attack through the Ardennes was nearly impossible, so they had left the region relatively unguarded. But this attack would be a dangerous gamble because the German forces would be extremely vulnerable to a counterattack from the north. Hitler was convinced, however, that the element of surprise would give Germany the critical edge. Once the Germans pushed through the forest into France, they would threaten to cut off from behind the entire British and French armies in northern Belgium. Hitler's brilliant strategy would meet with astounding success.

The German offensive against the Allies began on May 10, 1940. The German forces in the north moved swiftly through the

Erwin Rommel and his staff discuss routes through France in this 1940 photograph. German troops crushed French defenses within three days.

Blitzkrieg

Blitzkrieg, or "lightning war," was the most important German strategic innovation of the war. Although a German word, the term was popularized in 1939 by Western reporters. They needed a catchy phrase to describe the speed and destructiveness of the German attack against Poland.

A blitzkrieg featured a coordinated attack by airplanes, tanks, and motorized infantry. Speed was the key to success. John Keegan, a British military historian, writes: "Tanks of a panzer division would surge ahead, bypassing the enemy's strong points, to penetrate deep behind the lines and cut up the troops into separate pockets. Dive-bombers gave the tanks air cover. Slow-moving conventional artillery and infantry followed up to crush the pockets."

In the first half of the war, the Germans enjoyed remarkable success with the blitzkrieg. The Allied armies were defeated in a matter of weeks, and millions of Soviet soldiers were taken prisoner. Later in the war, however, the Soviets learned to combat the strategy. They would entice the attacking Germans forward and then launch devastating counterattacks from the wings.

Stuka *dive-bombers gave German tanks the air cover they needed to penetrate deep behind Allied lines.*

Netherlands and drove out the Belgian troops. Fifty infantry divisions and seven panzer units with more than twenty-two hundred tanks drove into the Ardennes Forest and achieved complete surprise. The panzer divisions faced only three French infantry divisions and three hundred tanks in their path through the forest. German dive-bombers *(Stukas)* terrorized the French troops, which fled in retreat. Large numbers of French soldiers were so demoralized that they even surrendered voluntarily. On May 12, the Germans crossed the French border and within three days, they had totally crushed the French defenses. The German forces then wheeled northward, toward the coast to cut off the Allied forces in Belgium. The Germans' next move would be to encircle the British and French forces.

"Blood, Toil, Tears and Sweat"

On May 10, Winston Churchill replaced Chamberlain as British prime minister. Three days later, Churchill spoke before the House of Commons, in the first of a series of speeches that inspired the nation. "I have nothing to offer but blood, toil, tears and sweat," Churchill said, but he promised "victory, however long and hard the road may be." Churchill flew to Paris on May 15 to meet with Gen. Maurice-Gustave Gamelin, the chief of staff, and French premier Paul Reynaud, who told Churchill: "We are beaten. We have lost the battle." Churchill asked Gamelin where his reserve troops were because they were needed to fight the oncoming Germans. Gamelin shrugged his shoulders and told Churchill there were none. Churchill now had no other option and began to evacuate his British forces.

The port of Dunkerque, smoldering in the aftermath of battle, was the scene of a dramatic rescue that became a symbol of British determination and courage.

On May 25, the British army started to retreat to the French coast. The day before, Hitler had ordered his panzer divisions to halt their attack for two days. By the time he withdrew his order, it was too late to overwhelm the British forces. British troops set up defenses around the port of Dunkerque. They fought courageously to give their fellow troops enough time to escape. The British government demanded the use of any vessel more than thirty feet long that could float to help the forces escape. A bizarre assortment of barges, fishing boats, pleasure boats, cabin steamers, and destroyers was assembled. The ships made their way across the English Channel to ferry the troops back to Great Britain. The weary soldiers stood on the beaches in long, winding lines, awaiting their turn to board. They then waded out to the ships in neck-deep water. German planes periodically swept the beach with machine-gun fire and torpedoed the ships. Thirty warships and 665 small boats were sunk. Yet the improvised rescue saved 335,000 Allied soldiers, including almost the entire British army and some 100,000 French troops, in just ten days.

The rescue turned a crushing military defeat into a rousing psychological victory. Dunkerque became a symbol of British determination and courage. It gave the British the will to fight on. In the days following the rescue, Churchill proclaimed: "We shall fight on the beaches, we shall fight on the landing grounds, we shall fight in the fields and the streets, we shall fight in the hills, we shall never surrender."

The French army still had 50 divisions to form a new front, but they were opposed by 130 German divisions. When the Germans launched their attack on France on June 5, French soldiers again quickly retreated. Only troops commanded by the young general Charles de Gaulle put up any spirited resistance. Thousands of beaten French troops were marched slowly off to prison camps. Marshal Philippe Petain, the seventy-nine-year-old French military hero of World War I who had been named deputy prime minister, announced he would call a truce with the Germans rather than continue fighting. Under the terms of this armistice, Germany occupied northern France and a collaborating French government, led by Petain, controlled southern France.

On June 14, 1940, the triumphant German army raised the Nazi swastika flag on the Eiffel Tower in Paris. French citizens and World War I veterans wept openly at the sight of German troops marching down their streets. De Gaulle, who escaped to England, broadcast a message from London on June 18. "This war is a world war," he said. "Whatever happens, the flame of resistance must not and will not be extinguished." He urged French citizens to continue the fight against the Germans. And as Churchill said: "The Battle of France is over. I expect that the Battle of Britain is about to begin."

Hitler poses in front of the Eiffel Tower in Paris in June 1940 (above), just days after his army raised the Nazi flag over this French landmark; a Frenchman weeps (below) as German soldiers march into the French capital.

CHAPTER TWO

Hitler's Drive for Total Victory

H itler's triumph was unparalleled in European history. It had taken Napoleon ten years and three different military campaigns to gain control of Europe. Hitler had captured the continent in little more than three months of fighting. It seemed that the mighty German war machine could not be defeated.

Yet the war was not over by any means. Great Britain may have been humbled by its retreat at Dunkerque, but it remained defiant. The Soviet Union was still formally at peace with Nazi Germany, but there was no question that Hitler intended to battle the country in the near future. The biggest question concerned the United States: would it come to the aid of Great Britain or maintain its official policy of neutrality? Hitler's long-term goal had always been to absolutely dominate Europe. This required the decisive defeat of Great Britain and the Soviet Union. He fully realized, though, that the American entry into the war on the side of Great Britain could make this impossible. Therefore, Hitler wanted to conquer Great Britain and the Soviet Union before the power of the United States could tilt the balance in the Allies' favor.

During the next eighteen months, Hitler would attempt to achieve his dream of total victory. But, by the end of 1941, he had not yet conquered Europe, and the European war had been transformed into a world war. All the great powers—the United States, the Soviet Union, and Great Britain—were aligned against Nazi Germany.

In June 1940, however, Great Britain stood alone, besieged by one of the strongest military forces in history. Churchill, after

Dunkerque, had promised that the British would never give up the fight. Nevertheless, Hitler was convinced that he could reach a compromise agreement with Churchill. While the French armistice was being negotiated, he told an assistant: "The British have lost the war, but they don't know it; one must give them time, and they will come around." Hitler saw no reason why Great Britain should continue fighting against such terrible odds when a compromise would leave the country unharmed and free. Hitler's peace terms were straightforward: Germany would not interfere with the British colonial empire, but Great Britain would recognize Germany's domination over the continent. With Britain out of the way, Hitler would then have a free hand to engage in "the mortal conflict with Russia." He was so confident that Great Britain would accept the peace terms that he had made very few preparations for a potential invasion of England. As of early July, the German military had not drawn up any plans to invade and had made no attempt to gather any of the necessary landing craft.

Certain British cabinet members recommended accepting an armistice, but Churchill refused. Great Britain would continue fighting the war unless Germany surrendered all of its war gains and gave guarantees to respect the sovereignty, or freedom and independence, of its neighbors. Because Churchill did not believe that Hitler would turn back from his dream of empire, he rejected the Nazi leader's terms. "Let us therefore brace ourselves to our duties," he told the House of Commons, "and so bear ourselves that if the British Empire and its Commonwealth last for a thousand years, men will say: 'this was their finest hour.'"

The Battle of Britain

Hitler ordered his general staff in late July to develop a plan, code-named Operation Sea Lion, to invade England. The German army contemplated landing 250,000 soldiers on the southern shores of England, but its military commanders were well aware that the German navy could not carry out the invasion anytime during the summer. Its fleet had been reduced in an early campaign in Norway, and sufficient landing craft and vessels had not yet been assembled. The German generals told Hitler that September 15 was the earliest date that Operation Sea Lion could begin.

In the meantime, Hitler assigned the Luftwaffe a momentous task. Before the invasion, Hitler wanted the German air force to pound Britain with around-the-clock bombing. The Battle of Britain, as the air campaign became known, was a historic conflict. For the first time in warfare, an air force alone attempted to break the enemy's will and capacity to resist. In previous wars, victory had always resulted from one of two factors. One was

Winston Churchill

Winston Churchill, the British statesman and author, was born in November 1874 in Oxfordshire, England. His father was Lord Randolph Churchill, a prominent figure in the Conservative party. Churchill was elected a member of Parliament in 1900. He was a shrewd opportunist who, in his political career, was not above switching parties when it gave him an advantage.

He served as head of the British navy during World War I but was forced to resign his post in 1915, after the disastrous British landing at Gallipoli. Between the wars, Churchill continued serving in the House of Commons. He also devoted time to his writing, publishing several historical works. He became prime minister in May 1940. Churchill served in that capacity again after World War II from 1951 to 1955.

Churchill could be recognized by his gravelly voice, his ever-present cigar, and his two-fingered "V for victory" salute. Churchill loved power and was a bit of a show-off. As prime minister, he frequently and deliberately took great personal risks, such as walking around London in the midst of heavy German bombing raids. An eloquent speaker, Churchill was also a master of the written word. At the end of his career, he published his memoirs of World War II in a six-volume work, entitled *The Second World War*. For this and other writings, Churchill was awarded the Nobel Prize for literature in 1953.

Winston Churchill, Great Britain's prime minister during World War II, was an eloquent speaker, writer, and statesman.

British firefighters prepare for war on home soil (left) and anti-aircraft guns are tested in Hyde Park (right) in war exercises conducted in London in 1939.

naval superiority. This meant that if an island nation like Great Britain maintained a strong navy, it would be invulnerable to attack. The other factor was a superiority in ground forces that could occupy another nation's territory. Now, Germany's strategists believed the Luftwaffe, without help from the navy or army, could bring Great Britain to its knees and make an invasion unnecessary.

It was a battle between two superbly matched opponents. Against the German Messerschmitt fighters and heavy bombers, the British Fighter Command used their Spitfires and Hurricane fighters. The fighter planes were evenly matched in speed and firepower. The Germans had more planes, but this advantage was misleading. Bombers could only operate successfully if protected by fighter planes, and the two countries had nearly the same number of fighter planes. The British enjoyed two distinct advantages. Their chain of radar stations gave them advance warning of the German attacks. From the time German aircraft took off from their bases in France, they were spotted on British radar screens, so the Royal Air Force (RAF) command could communicate to their fighters where to attack. The British also had the good fortune of fighting on their home territory. German pilots who were shot down over Great Britain were either killed or captured. On the other hand, British pilots bailed out over friendly territory and could rejoin their units almost immediately. Whereas German pilots had to worry constantly about a dwindling fuel supply, the British could refuel at any number of airfields. Britain's main disadvantage was its shortage of trained pilots, and this would prove critical at the height of the battle.

On July 10, German bombers, escorted by fighter planes, crossed the English Channel to begin the Battle of Britain. The

The Wonder of Radar

The British invention of radar was one of the most closely guarded secrets of the war. It gave them a critical tactical advantage during the Battle of Britain. With radar, British fighter command had advance warning of the approach of German bombers and fighters.

The British system consisted of fifty radar stations lining the coast of England. A three-hundred-foot-tall steel mast was the only sign of these installations. Radar works by transmitting radio signals that bounce back when they are reflected against objects in the sky. The signals are then picked up by the radar stations and displayed as blips on monitors. The radar blips measure the exact height, bearing, distance, and number of approaching enemy aircraft.

When German bombers were detected, the precise details of the incoming raid were telephoned to an operation room. Inside, members of the Women's Air Force Auxiliary Corps (WAAC) busily plotted the battle on flat tables. Markers representing friendly and enemy aircraft were shifted across the table to indicate the changing progress of the battle. Overhead, the generals could see every detail of the conflict developing beneath them. The operation rooms were also directly linked to the sounds of the war through the pilots' radios. The entire room would become deathly silent whenever a pilot got into trouble. On many occasions, they listened sadly to the anguished cries of a pilot burning to death in the cockpit.

Radar gave the British military a critical tactical advantage during the Battle of Britain.

Germans initially concentrated on destroying the British navy, which was the key defense against an invasion. They attacked navy docks and bases, but their bombing was surprisingly inaccurate. After three weeks, the Royal Navy was largely untouched. During the second stage of the attack in August, the Germans concentrated on destroying RAF airfields in southwestern England. On August 15, the Germans attacked with eighteen hundred planes. Squadrons of Spitfires and Hurricanes were sent up to meet them, and a gigantic battle raged in the sky for hours. At the end of the day, the RAF was bruised and weary, but it was still flying. The British lost thirty-nine planes and the Germans lost seventy-five. On the following day, the Germans launched seventeen hundred planes in another punishing raid. During the next three weeks, the Luftwaffe sent an average of one thousand planes across the channel each day, with wave after wave of bombers pounding the RAF bases.

Hermann Göring, a Nazi official, bragged that the British were being brought to their knees by Nazi air power.

RAF on the Ropes

The Germans attempted only a handful of attacks on the British radar network. The British stations were especially vulnerable because the control rooms were located aboveground in poorly camouflaged wooden huts, where any direct hit could destroy them. The German bombers, however, concentrated on knocking out the radar towers themselves and ignored the control rooms, believing that the towers were more important. The Germans were also careful to avoid direct attacks on London. Hitler feared the British would retaliate by attacking German cities.

Although the RAF put up a brave fight, the sheer number of German planes began to slowly crush the British defenses. Hermann Göring, a Nazi official, bragged that the British were being brought to their knees by the air power of the Luftwaffe. His boasts were not far off the mark. Seven airfields and five ground stations were completely knocked out. The elaborate British communication and control system stood on the verge of collapse. More planes were being lost than could be built by the aircraft factories. The fighting took a heavy toll on the pilots as well. By late August, the RAF was beginning to run out of pilots and was forced to enlist inexperienced recruits. The British recruited a multinational volunteer force of Czechs, Poles, Canadians, Australians, Frenchmen, and even seven Americans. Eighteen-year-olds were sent into combat with only ten hours of training. Many died before they really learned how to fly.

The RAF pilots had a grueling life. Pilots were on alert twelve hours a day, and many flew as many as six missions a day. In rare quiet moments, they sat around the air bases reading or playing cards. As soon as the siren sounded to warn of a coming attack, they ran to their planes and took off within minutes.

Many buildings lay in ruins after firebombs and high explosives rained on London for many hours during one all-night raid.

Once in the air, they were in radio contact with ground controllers who directed them toward the incoming German planes. As the German bombers came in, British fighters swooped down to attack. Spectacular dogfights raged in the sky, leaving wildly swirling vapor trails in their wake. Dogfights rarely lasted more than fifteen minutes, but in this kind of combat, that could seem like a lifetime. Pilots had to make split-second decisions that often meant the difference between life and death. Pilots learned to use the sky and sun to their advantage, keeping the sun behind them and using cloud cover to hide from enemy planes. Their greatest advantage, however, was their own boldness. For example, one British pilot was surrounded by two German fighters. He flew straight at them at top speed, daring the Germans to pull away for fear of colliding. He purposely created a glancing midair collision that downed one German plane and sent the other scurrying back across the channel, undoubtedly muttering about the crazy British tactics. The pilot then flew his own damaged plane back to his home base.

When their missions were completed, the pilots returned home to see how many of their buddies had survived. When darkness fell, the pilots hurried into London to a nightclub or a theater performance. The RAF pilots were astonishingly young, most no more than twenty-three years old. They were good-looking, dashing men who seemed to lead glamorous and exciting lives. They gained notorious reputations for their all-night parties. They appeared to have an endless supply of girlfriends. At first, they were convinced of their own invincibility and immortality. Yet as the weeks of fighting continued, their morale disintegrated. More and more of their fellow pilots were killed or wounded. The shadow of death crept over every mission. Each pilot wondered if he would survive another day. One squadron leader, on the verge of a brief vacation in late August, wrote: "I was convinced that we were beaten, that we had lost the Battle. I was fantastically tired and utterly depressed. My squadron had been in heavy fighting since May without a break. I left it, I thought, a very depleted and thoroughly beaten fighting unit."

By late August, the very survival of the British Fighter Command was indeed at risk. The head of the RAF, Air Marshal Dowding, admitted, "What we need is a miracle." Fortunately, for the British, they were handed one by Hitler himself. On August 22, the Luftwaffe mistakenly bombed London. As a result, Churchill sent the RAF on a series of bombing raids against Berlin. Although the raids caused only twenty-nine casualties, the effect on German morale was devastating. Hitler had assured the German people that their capital would never be touched. The Nazi leader was outraged and vowed to raze Great Britain's cities to the ground. On Hitler's personal order, the Luftwaffe switched its tactics and began full-scale terror attacks on London. This would prove to be a fatal mistake. If the Luftwaffe had expanded its attacks on the airfields, the RAF defenses might have collapsed. By attacking London, the Germans gave the British the chance to rebuild the airfields and increase their aircraft production.

The Blitz Begins

Day after day in September 1940, the horizon over England was filled with German planes heading to London. The Germans dropped tons of explosives and bombs. Huge fires broke out throughout the city. All over London, buckets of sand and tanks of water were gathered to fight the fires. Citizens took shelter in store basements, bank vaults, and subway stations. There was continual antiaircraft fire. In the first week, twenty-five hundred British were killed and ten thousand were wounded. More than forty thousand would die in the terror-bombing campaign.

The climax of the battle came on September 15. The Germans sent two hundred bombers against London. The British mobilized every available plane and mounted a spirited counterattack. Furious dogfights raged in the clear blue sky the entire day. The first wave of Germans was beaten back, as was a second wave in the late afternoon. At the end of the day, the British had not been beaten, and the Battle of Britain was effectively over. Afterward, German bombers switched to destructive, but strategically ineffective, night raids against London. This phase was called the "blitz" by Londoners.

The battle was a crushing blow for the Germans. Hitler was forced to admit that the Luftwaffe had failed to either destroy the British air force or break the British will to resist. Without naval or air superiority, Germany was helpless to invade England. Without an invasion, there could be no swift end to the war. On

Three children sit in the wreckage of their suburban London home.

The dome of St. Paul's Cathedral in London rises through the thick smoke and flames left in the wake of bombing.

Life Under the Blitz

During the "blitz," the German air force attempted the systematic destruction of England's cities. Every night, for fifty-seven consecutive days, German planes dropped bombs, explosives, and land mines on London, Manchester, Liverpool, Southampton, and other cities. Thirty thousand civilians were killed in the campaign, and 3.5 million homes were damaged or destroyed. The Germans expected British morale to collapse under the strain of the attack, but the British remained defiant.

Every night, a warning siren heralded the approach of the German bombers. Searchlights crisscrossed the skies, suddenly capturing a bomber in the spotlight. Once a plane was spotted, antiaircraft batteries would fire. A stream of bright fire exploded in the sky. Barrage balloons, lifted on steel cables, forced the German planes to fly at greater heights, which meant their bombing was less accurate. When the bombs fell, entire city streets disappeared, and blocks burst into raging flames. People were crushed beneath falling buildings or burned to death in fires. Huge infernos burned out of control every night, casting a strange light over the city. People went on their rooftops to look out, and although there were no lights on anywhere, it almost seemed as if it were daytime.

Londoners, as one observer remarked, became twentieth-century cave dwellers. As soon as the sirens roared, millions headed for shelter below ground, such as public bomb shelters or bank vaults. The underground, London's subway system, was one of the most popular sites. Every inch of the subway platforms was jammed with people, their blankets, food, and drink. The conditions were incredibly claustrophobic. People had no room to stretch their legs, the bathrooms were overcrowded, and the incessant pounding of the bombs wore on peoples' nerves. Londoners played cards or chess and sang songs to make the time pass faster. In subway stations near London's theater district, stars like Laurence Olivier and Vivien Leigh would come down after their evening shows and perform impromptu skits and songs for the crowds.

People would emerge at dawn after the all-clear signal sounded. Many returned home to find nothing but a pile of bricks and wood where the house used to stand. Rescue crews and fire fighters dug through the rubble of buildings looking for trapped survivors. Londoners bore the hardships and suffering with great courage and humor. A common lapel button read: "Don't tell me, I've got a bomb story too." Churchill often traveled around the city, visiting bombed-out areas. On one visit, he recalled: "In my life, I have never been treated with so much kindness as by the people who have suffered most. One would have thought I had brought them some fine substantial benefit which improved their lot in life…. When we got back into the car, a harsher mood swept over the haggard crowd. 'Give it to 'em back' they cried, and 'Let them have it too.'"

A sign warns passersby to stay clear of an unexploded 2,500-pound German bomb that fell on a London street.

September 17, 1940, Hitler announced that Operation Sea Lion would be postponed until the following spring.

The Battle of Britain was truly a heroic fight. The twenty-five hundred young pilots of the British Fighter Command had single-handedly altered the course of World War II. In Churchill's immortal words, "Never in the field of human conflict was so much owed by so many to so few."

America on the Verge of War

Although Great Britain had been saved for the moment, its long-term security was still in jeopardy. Already, Germany's dreaded submarines, called U-boats, were terrorizing Britain's merchant fleet and threatening its precious lifeline of supplies from the outside world. Furthermore, Churchill feared Hitler might try to invade again in the spring of 1941. The only way Britain could survive, was by convincing the United States to enter the war. "I can see only one recourse," Churchill told his son. "We must get the Americans in."

When Europe plunged into war, the United States did not want to get involved in European conflicts. Ever since World War I, Americans believed the United States should avoid playing a role in European politics. These isolationists supported a policy of strict neutrality and noninterference in the affairs of other countries. In support of this attitude, Congress passed the Neutrality Acts from 1935 to 1937, which prohibited the president from providing military assistance to nations at war. Little money had been spent on the country's own armed services. By the late 1930s, the United States had only the thirty-ninth largest army in the world.

The America First Committee, whose leading spokesman was the famous aviator Charles Lindbergh, the first pilot to fly across the Atlantic, promoted the isolationist cause. America First argued that a war in Europe did not affect American interests. The country therefore should stay out of the conflict. These opinions were so widespread in the 1930s that President Franklin Roosevelt was forced to promise publicly that American troops would be sent abroad only in case of an attack on the United States itself.

There were some groups, however, that enthusiastically supported American participation in the world community. They felt that the economic and political interests of the United States were threatened by the growing power of Nazi Germany. These internationalists were strongly idealistic, and they believed the United States should oppose the Nazis in a show of support for freedom and democracy. The internationalists believed that U.S. military and moral support should be given to all democratic governments.

The president, too, was in favor of aiding Europe. Russell Freedman writes, "Franklin Roosevelt was an internationalist by virtue of his education, family background and personal convictions."

Franklin Roosevelt

Franklin Delano Roosevelt, or FDR, was born in Hyde Park, New York, on January 30, 1882. He served as president for more than twelve years, longer than any other president. He was the only person elected to four separate terms. He led the United States through its most troubled economic period and through World War II. Along with Abraham Lincoln, who also guided the nation through perilous times, Roosevelt is considered by many to be one of the greatest presidents in American history.

Roosevelt grew up in a wealthy family but entered politics because he wanted to contribute his talents to the public service. Before he was elected president, Roosevelt enjoyed a long and distinguished career, serving as an assistant secretary to the U.S. Navy, as a New York state senator, and as governor of New York. In 1921, Roosevelt contracted polio, which left him partially crippled for the rest of his life. Although many expected him to abandon politics, Roosevelt refused to change his life because of his disability. He learned to walk with the aid of leg braces and crutches and lived a full and active life. He married his cousin Eleanor Roosevelt, who became a distinguished public figure in her own right, and together they had six children.

FDR was elected president in 1932 and took office in the midst of an economic catastrophe. The Great Depression, which occurred after the collapse of the stock market in October 1929, left millions unemployed and homeless. The nation's banks and industries were in total disarray. The first one hundred days of Roosevelt's administration were a period of breathtaking activity that lifted the nation's spirits. His programs, which FDR called the New Deal, put millions to work and revitalized the American economy. Roosevelt also introduced many innovative programs that improved the life of ordinary Americans. The minimum wage, unemployment insurance, Social Security, and the right to form trade unions were all developed during his presidency.

Roosevelt was an exceptional president, with great political skill and intelligence. He was a great speaker who regularly addressed the American people on the radio in "fireside chats." These were relaxed, easygoing speeches that gave listeners the impression that the president was speaking to them from his own living room.

President Franklin Roosevelt exhibited great political skill and intelligence during his years in office.

As early as 1937, President Roosevelt warned that the rise of Nazi Germany threatened not just its European neighbors but all nations on earth. "Innocent nations are being sacrificed to a greed for power," he said. "If these things come to pass in other parts of the world, let no one imagine that America will escape, that America may expect mercy, that the Western Hemisphere will not be attacked." In private, FDR confided to his personal advisers that he believed the United States would have no choice but to go to war in the coming years.

Roosevelt was also a shrewd politician and realized that in 1938 Americans would not yet see a need to get involved in European politics. It was only after the fall of France in June 1940 that American public opinion began to shift. Americans worried that if Great Britain were to fall also, then the United States would stand alone. By the summer of 1941, most Americans fully expected to be at war in the near future. A Gallup poll showed 85 percent believed the country would be drawn into the European war. In the same poll, a substantial majority also stated they felt it was more important for Germany to be defeated than for the United States to stay out of the war. Americans did not want war, but they overwhelmingly supported FDR's policies every step of the way.

In June 1940, Roosevelt petitioned Congress to revise the Neutrality Acts so that the United States could begin aiding Britain. He also called for the modernization of U.S. armed forces and war industries to ensure that the country would be an "arsenal of democracy." In March 1941, Roosevelt's Lend-Lease Act was passed by Congress. The act allowed the United States to lend or lease military equipment to Great Britain and other Allies in return for the promise of repayment after the war. During the course of the war, military and economic aid worth fifty million dollars was given to the Allies.

In August 1941, Roosevelt met with Churchill on a naval destroyer off the coast of Newfoundland, Canada. It was the first of their many wartime conferences. The two leaders issued a joint declaration, known as the Atlantic Charter, that committed their respective countries to creating a multinational democratic alliance to crush aggression. Although it stopped short of a formal declaration of war against Nazi Germany, it was a clear statement of U.S. intent to aid the Allies. The United States was not yet at war, but its fate now seemed permanently linked with that of the British.

Hitler's Obsession

As the Americans and British grew closer, Hitler's emphasis shifted away from Great Britain back to the Soviet Union. Hitler's general staff warned against an attack on the Soviet Union. The

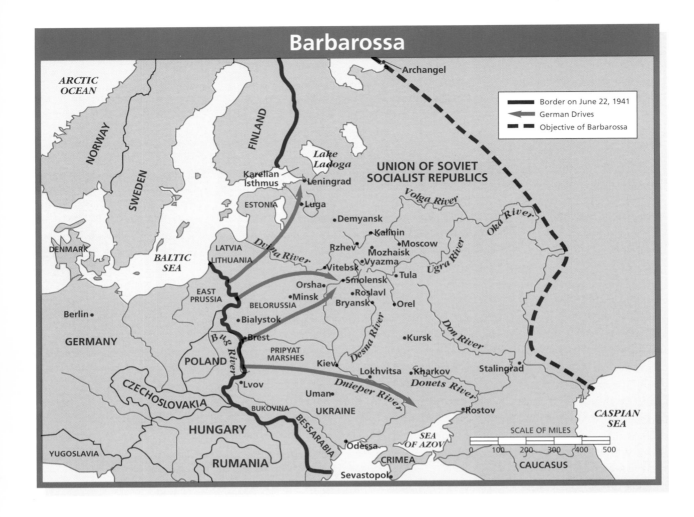

Barbarossa

Legend:
- ▬▬ Border on June 22, 1941
- ← German Drives
- ▬ ▬ Objective of Barbarossa

difficulties of invading such an immense country should not be underestimated, they said. And they cautioned against fighting a war on two fronts. They especially feared a repeat of Napoleon's defeat in 1812, when his French army was forced to retreat because of Russia's brutal winter weather. Despite these warnings, an invasion of the Soviet Union was the key to Hitler's long-term and short-term goals.

On the one hand, the invasion was the logical consequence of the beliefs Hitler had stated for more than twenty years. His political career had always been dedicated to destroying world communism. The downfall of the Soviet Union would also solve his long-term obsession of providing more *Lebensraum,* or "living space," for the Germans. The vast Soviet territories could be colonized by the Germans, and their agricultural lands would feed the entire German empire. In short, the conquest of the Soviet Union was the only way to ensure Germany's domination of Europe.

Hitler also believed the invasion made good sense in the short run. Once the Soviet Union was defeated, Hitler was sure the British would have no choice but to agree to a negotiated peace. An attack on the Soviets would also be a preventive strike against the Soviet Red Army before it was prepared and equipped to fight. Above all, Hitler believed that the Germans would have an easy victory. "Just kick in the door and the whole rotten structure will collapse," Hitler said.

Plans for the invasion, code-named Barbarossa after the nickname of the medieval emperor Frederick I, were finalized in early 1941. The campaign would begin in the spring of 1941. Four million soldiers were assembled, along with thousands of tanks and artillery. Three army groups would move separately toward Leningrad, Moscow, and Kiev. Their immediate priority was to capture Moscow as quickly as possible. The Soviet capital was the center of Stalin's authority and power. Its downfall would ensure Germany's victory. The German invasion would prove to be one of the most important events of the entire war. For the next four years, the Soviet Union would engage the bulk of Germany's military might. And the Soviet ability to hold on gave the American entry into the war such decisive importance.

On the eve of Operation Barbarossa, none of the Allies expected that the Soviets would be able to last more than a few months. The Soviet Union was woefully unprepared for war. Although the Red Army was the largest force in the world, with five million men in uniform and another eight million in reserve, it was ill equipped and poorly led. The Soviets still used horses to transport supplies, their airplanes were hopelessly outdated, and only one-quarter of their admittedly inferior tanks were in working order. Thirty-five thousand senior army officers had been killed by Stalin during his reign of terror in the 1930s. The new commanders were untested and lacked military expertise. Stalin himself foolishly disregarded warnings, from his own spies and British intelligence, that a German invasion was being

German troops invaded the Soviet Union in 1941. Although Soviet troops were unprepared, the fight lasted four years.

German tanks rolled rapidly across the Soviet countryside despite fierce resistance from Soviet soldiers.

The Nazis controlled a huge chunk of the eastern Soviet Union and came within eighteen miles of Moscow in 1941.

Muddy roads posed only a minor obstacle for German tanks pushing into the heart of the Soviet Union (left). A Soviet soldier hurls grenades at German tanks (right).

planned. On June 21, a German deserter told Soviet officers that the invasion would begin the following morning. Stalin refused to issue a warning order or to alert troops on the border. His failure to grasp reality would be extremely costly for the Red Army.

At 3:15 on the morning of June 22, 1941, the German attack began. The still night exploded into the thunder and lightning of countless artillery barrages. German troops moved under cover of this wall of fire. The Luftwaffe caught the Soviet air force completely off guard, destroying twelve hundred aircraft on the ground. Tank divisions drove forward at a rapid pace. In the first few days, many panzer units advanced more than one hundred miles. Within a week, the German army stood on the verge of encircling four Soviet armies. The initial German success was astounding. By August, almost 2 million Soviet soldiers had been taken prisoner and another 1.5 million killed or wounded. The Nazis controlled the easternmost five hundred miles of the Soviet Union and were only two hundred miles from Moscow. Another terror was the special SS units that traveled behind the advancing troops. Their heinous mission was to execute all Soviet Jews in the German-controlled territories. Two million Jews were murdered in these abominable operations between June and November 1941.

Despite their staggering losses, the Soviet soldiers fought with bravery and courage. They had a strong loyalty to their country. They also feared being imprisoned more than they did dying on the battlefield. The fighting on the eastern front was incredibly savage and brutal. German soldiers, following Hitler's orders, massacred Soviet prisoners of war and tortured and mistreated soldiers and civilians. Of the 5.7 million Soviet soldiers taken prisoner during the war, 3.3 million died in captivity. Red Army troops also feared their own leaders. Soviet soldiers captured by

Soviet soldiers donned felt boots and warm parkas as winter approached. The boots and clothing of German soldiers could not hold up against the harsh Soviet winter.

the Germans were declared traitors by Stalin. Even if they escaped and returned to the Soviet lines, they were likely to be imprisoned and shot. Similarly, commanders who attempted to retreat were accused of treachery and executed.

A Stab at Total Victory

As city after city fell to the onrushing Germans, the German generals were convinced that total victory lay in their grasp. An immediate advance on Moscow would wipe out what was left of the Red Army. Any delay in mounting an attack on the capital would give the Soviets time to regroup and ready stronger defenses. Yet for the first time in the war, Hitler openly disregarded the advice of his generals and took personal direction of the campaign. He was obsessed with conquering more territory and capturing the resource-rich Ukraine. Hitler diverted panzer units to the south to aid in the encirclement of Kiev. Although the capture of the city was another stunning success—one million Soviets were killed, wounded, or taken prisoner—a month passed before the Moscow offensive was underway.

By the time the final assault on Moscow was back on track, weather conditions had deteriorated. The first snowfall in October left the dirt roads a muddy mess. Trucks and jeeps were mired in the thick mud. The constant snow, sleet, and bitter cold drained the soldiers. The German army had also suffered terrible losses. The dead and wounded totaled one-half million. As supplies of fuel, food, and ammunition grew scarce, the German advance soon slowed to a crawl, a mere two miles a day.

In Moscow, Marshal Georgy Zhukov rallied the city's defenses. Women and elderly men were assembled into work battalions to dig antitank ditches and trenches. In a feverish effort to save the city, 250,000 citizens labored for six weeks, constructing more than one hundred miles of fortifications. The Soviets also took the precaution of evacuating the diplomatic corps and government offices several hundred miles to the east.

By mid-November, the first frosts hardened the ground, making it possible for the Germans to begin their final assault on the capital. The Germans reached within eighteen miles of Moscow. An advance unit was close enough to spot the golden domes of the Kremlin. But the Soviet defenses held fast, and the German attack stalled on the outskirts of the city. The harsh Soviet winter was now upon them, and temperatures fell as low as minus forty degrees Fahrenheit. The German generals' greatest fear had become a reality. Their troops had not been given winter gear because Hitler did not want his soldiers to doubt that they would conquer the Soviet Union before the winter set in, and their boots and clothing disintegrated. The Germans stuck newspapers and propaganda pamphlets inside their boots and uniforms to keep warm. Frostbite casualties mounted steadily. The bitter cold sapped the German soldiers of the will to fight. They could go no farther. The German generals begged Hitler to allow the army to retreat to positions that were easier to defend, but he refused. He ordered his troops to dig in and hold every inch of Soviet territory that they had gained.

In late November, Stalin shifted ten divisions and one thousand tanks from their Far East posts to the eastern front. With these reinforcements, the Red Army now equalled the Germans in troops and equipment. Soviet troops were outfitted with felt boots and warm parkas and were accustomed to the freezing conditions. The Soviets had also recently begun receiving supplies of their new tank, the T-34, which proved to be the finest in the war. With these fortifications, the Red Army, on December 5, 1941, counterattacked along a broad six-hundred-mile front. By Christmas Day, they had pushed the German front line back forty miles. Operation Barbarossa failed in its major objectives. Neither Moscow nor Leningrad had fallen, and Stalin's government was still in power. Most important, by holding on despite its early defeats and then driving the Germans back, the Red Army shattered the German army's myth of invincibility once and for all. Hitler's attempt to bring a quick and decisive end to the war was a failure.

CHAPTER THREE

The Tide Turns

The course of the war was decisively changed by the events of December 7, 1941. This date became permanently etched in the American memory. Americans in the 1940s remember December 7 in the same way a different generation, two decades later, would remember where they were or what they were doing when President John Kennedy was assassinated. It was on December 7 that Japan, who had joined Germany and Italy in the war, launched a surprise attack against the American forces at Pearl Harbor in Hawaii. The United States formally entered the war the next day. The European war had now become a world war.

With both Germany and Japan as enemies, President Roosevelt had to decide where to concentrate the war effort: in Europe or in the Pacific? After Pearl Harbor, most Americans overwhelmingly supported fighting the Japanese. Roosevelt's chief of staff, Gen. George C. Marshall, however, advised a "Germany first" policy. He reasoned that Nazi Germany was the greater military danger to the United States. He especially feared that the Nazis might develop a "secret weapon" that would make them unbeatable. Roosevelt agreed with Marshall. The bulk of the American forces, eight million men, was committed to fight Germany and Italy. The American navy was committed to the Pacific War with Japan.

While the U.S. entry into the war was indeed an important moment, the full impact of the American war effort would not be felt until 1943. But in 1942, the entire course of the war was transformed by two major defeats suffered by Nazi Germany.

President Franklin Roosevelt had to decide who posed the greater threat to the United States—Germany or Japan. He chose Germany.

The Japanese attack on Pearl Harbor, on December 7, 1941, pushed the United States into World War II.

The first was by the British army at Alamein in North Africa. The second was by the Soviet Red Army at a city called Stalingrad. Hitler's dream of a one-thousand-year empire was destroyed in the burning sands of the North African desert and the harsh winter snows of the Soviet Union. These battles marked the great turning point of World War II. After Alamein and Stalingrad, the tide of Nazi conquest was stemmed. Hitler would never regain the chance to take Europe.

The roots of the battle of Alamein lay in the first years of the war. The British had fought the Italians and the Germans in North Africa since 1940. The conflict in 1941 was dominated by the brilliant German general Erwin Rommel. Rommel was nicknamed the Desert Fox for his daring tactics. He seemed to have an unerring instinct for his opponent's weaknesses and for narrow escapes. In 1941, Rommel won a series of dazzling victories that drove the British Eighth Army across the desert. His main target was the vital British garrison of Tobruk in Libya. This deep-water port was seventy-five miles from the Egyptian border. Control of the garrison guaranteed that the British army would be regularly resupplied with food, fuel, ammunition, and equipment. The capture of Tobruk would be a great victory for the Germans because it would effectively cut off the British supplies.

For seven months, Rommel besieged the garrison. The British forces put up a stiff resistance. German propaganda described the British soldiers as "rats in a trap." The British troops began to refer to themselves proudly as the Rats of Tobruk. A British counterattack in November 1941 broke the siege and relieved the garrison. Rommel was driven back to his starting point of the previous February. By late 1941, both sides had reached a weary stalemate.

The USS Arizona *burns (left) and smoke billows and flames rise from the wreckage of the aerial attack on Pearl Harbor (right).*

The Secret War

Every nation, whether at war or during peacetime, seeks to discover the secrets of its enemies. During World War II, spies and code breakers performed invaluable services for the Allies. Their efforts were essential for the Allied victory.

Perhaps the most traditional component of the secret war is the use of spies. These men or women, living in occupied Europe or neutral countries, reported to the Allies about German military capabilities, troop movements, and battle plans. The Lucy spy ring in Switzerland and the Red Orchestra in France and Belgium were among the most effective secret agents.

Although not as glamorous as spying, code breaking actually became the greatest triumph of the secret war. Code breaking was the interception, decoding, and transcription of enemy radio messages. Each country took elaborate precautions to ensure that its radio traffic could not be understood by other nations. The German military used a coding machine, known as the "Enigma machine," to guard its radio messages. The machine looked like a cross between a portable typewriter and cash register. When a German operator typed a message into the machine, it was coded into a series of different letters that only another Enigma machine could decipher. The Germans were convinced that the Enigma code was unbreakable.

But this was not the case. Great Britain established a secret code-breaking operation at Bletchley Park, where it recruited the country's most brilliant mathematicians to crack the German code. Mistakes by inexperienced or lazy German code clerks in typing messages gave these mathematicians a pattern that they used to break the code. By 1942, the British were intercepting and decoding the German messages as soon as they were sent out.

The most important information that the British discovered was given the code name Ultra. This intelligence gave the Allies a critical advantage. They could follow German U-Boat movements. They learned of German troop positions before the battle of Alamein and other invasions. Sometimes, they even learned of entire German battle plans before the fighting took place. The Ultra intelligence was the greatest secret of the war. Only the top Allied generals and political leaders knew about it. It was not until twenty years after the war that Great Britain and the United States finally released information about the program to the public.

Governments used ciphering machines to break coded messages sent by the enemy.

The Nature of Desert Warfare

The battles in these early years were typical of the back-and-forth nature of desert warfare. Desert war was determined, above all, by geography and supply. Both the German and British armies were confined to fighting along a narrow coastal strip forty miles wide. This coastal region stretched fourteen hundred miles from Tripoli in Libya to Alexandria in Egypt. It was bordered on the north by the Mediterranean Sea and on the south by impassable desert. The only targets of military value were the ports that lay along the coast. A desert army's range was dictated by how much food, fuel, and water it could carry along. When supply lines were stretched so far that they could not provide enough food and water for the soldiers, an army had two choices. It could either withdraw back to its own lines or else move forward to capture the next available port. Desert fighting fell into a regular pattern. As soon as one army seized several ports and stretched its supply lines to the breaking point, the opponent would take the initiative and regain its lost ground. The British soldiers compared this inconclusive fighting to a horse race in which the horses are constantly overtaking each other. They nicknamed the desert battles the "Benghazi handicap" after the name of the long coastal road.

During the first six months of 1942, there was a lull in the fighting. Rommel renewed the German offensive in May. Within weeks, the British surrendered all the territory they had recently captured. They were forced to regroup to a defensive position near Alamein. The garrison at Tobruk was left behind once again. The British believed the stronghold could not be captured, but they had neglected to maintain its defenses. On June 21, 1942, after only a one-week siege, the British forces at Tobruk surrendered to Rommel's Afrika Korps.

German general Rommel (top, above) reaches Libya where one of his main targets was the British-controlled port of Tobruk. At right, Soviet soldiers dislodge German troops near Stalingrad.

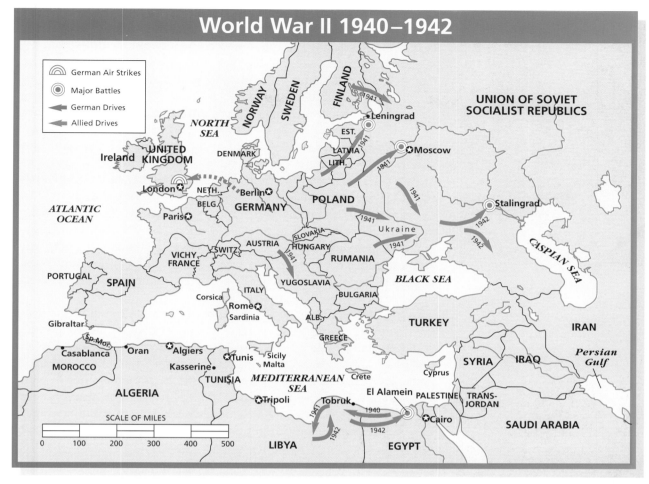

World War II 1940–1942

Legend:
- German Air Strikes
- Major Battles
- German Drives
- Allied Drives

Map labels include: NORTH SEA, NORWAY, SWEDEN, FINLAND, Leningrad, 1941, EST., LATVIA, LITH., Moscow, UNION OF SOVIET SOCIALIST REPUBLICS, Ireland, UNITED KINGDOM, DENMARK, London, NETH., Berlin, BELG., GERMANY, POLAND, 1941, Ukraine, 1941, Stalingrad, 1942, ATLANTIC OCEAN, Paris, SWITZ., AUSTRIA, SLOVAKIA, HUNGARY, RUMANIA, 1941, 1942, CASPIAN SEA, VICHY FRANCE, 1941, YUGOSLAVIA, BULGARIA, BLACK SEA, PORTUGAL, SPAIN, ITALY, Corsica, Rome, Sardinia, ALB., TURKEY, IRAN, Gibraltar, GREECE, Sp. Mor., Casablanca, Oran, Algiers, Tunis, Sicily, Malta, Crete, Cyprus, SYRIA, IRAQ, Persian Gulf, Kasserine, MOROCCO, TUNISIA, MEDITERRANEAN SEA, El Alamein, PALESTINE, TRANS-JORDAN, ALGERIA, Tripoli, Tobruk, 1940, 1941, 1942, Cairo, 1942, SAUDI ARABIA, LIBYA, EGYPT

SCALE OF MILES
0 100 200 300 400 500

The capture of Tobruk represented the height of German fortunes in World War II. The Germans gained valuable supplies and the road to Egypt now lay open. It appeared that nothing could prevent Rommel from conquering Egypt and then sweeping northeast to capture the Middle East oil fields. At the same time, German submarines were wreaking havoc with British and American shipping. On the eastern front, the German offensive in the spring had met with stunning success. Hitler boasted to his generals that the war was almost won, but the decisive battles were just ahead.

The Battle of Alamein

After the defeat at Tobruk, Churchill decided that his Eighth Army required a general with the same killer instinct as Rommel. In August, he named Lt. Gen. Bernard Montgomery to command the British forces. Montgomery would prove to be a worthy opponent of the Desert Fox. The British established a strong defensive position at Alamein, but Montgomery had no intention

British Lt. Gen. Bernard Montgomery advances against Rommel in North Africa.

British soldiers keep watch near Alamein.

of remaining on the defensive. He decided to put an end to the cat-and-mouse fighting between the two forces and designed a battle plan to destroy Rommel's forces once and for all.

Rommel made several unsuccessful attempts to penetrate the British lines. His troops were tired and his supplies almost completely exhausted. They were also greatly outnumbered by the British, who fielded 230,000 men and fourteen hundred tanks against the Germans' 80,000 troops and three hundred tanks. Rommel had no choice but to take the defensive. He established strong defenses atop the two ridges running from the coast to the vast desert known as the Qattara Depression. Rommel shielded his positions with a dense mine field. Over one-half million mines and booby traps were laid before the battle. This forty-mile line was called the "devil's garden" by the British troops. Still, the German forces were desperately short of supplies, ammunition, and tanks. Even worse, at the critical moment, they were left leaderless. Poor health forced Rommel to return to Germany on the eve of the battle.

On October 24, at 9:40 P.M., an earsplitting explosion disrupted the silent night. The sound of the British artillery barrage could be heard sixty miles away in Alexandria. The first British units to move forward were specially trained soldiers called sappers. They marked safe corridors through the mine fields with white tape and lanterns. Fifteen minutes later, the artillery fire abruptly stopped. There was a deathly silence on the battlefield. Five minutes later, another horrendous round of fire sounded. The British infantry began to move forward.

The first hours of the battle were incredibly bloody. German guns knocked out tanks and armored vehicles. The burning wrecks caused a massive bottleneck for the British forces in the rear. German bombs destroyed many of the white-taped corridors, so countless British soldiers stumbled into the mine field. Hidden machine-gun nests put out a murderous round of fire, and the British suffered heavy casualties. Several British commanders considered withdrawing, but Montgomery ordered the attack to continue. British troops mounted furious bayonet charges on the German positions. By dawn, some British units had gained a foothold atop the ridges.

Hitler ordered Rommel to leave his sickbed and fly to Alamein to resume command. He returned to find his army in complete disarray. Rommel ordered his panzer units to attack British-held positions on Kidney Ridge. Five successive attacks were beaten back. Before one last effort could be made, British airplanes bombarded the German troops for two horrible hours. The armored forces of the Afrika Korps were reduced to thirty tanks, which faced eight hundred British tanks. Rommel asked permission to retreat but was forbidden by Hitler. "There can be no other consideration, save that of holding fast, of not retreating

As the fight for Alamein raged in North Africa, Soviet soldiers took up positions against German forces advancing on another front, Stalingrad.

one step, of throwing every gun and every man into the battle," Hitler told Rommel. "You can show your troops no other way than that which leads to victory or death." On November 4, the British assault broke through the German lines and threatened Rommel's army with utter destruction. Rommel had no choice except to give the order to retreat. It marked the beginning of a long two-thousand mile retreat.

Alamein was a horrible defeat for Germany. The Afrika Korps lost fifty thousand men, almost half of its army. Its tank force was almost totally wiped out. Alamein was the first critical Allied victory over Germany, and Montgomery became the first British general to win a major battle against a German commander. "Before Alamein, we never had a victory," said Churchill. "After Alamein, we never had a defeat." In London, Churchill ordered the nation's church bells to ring on Sunday, November 15. It would be the first time they had tolled since 1940, when the bells were silenced except to warn of invasion.

Hitler's New Offensive in the East

While the fight for Alamein was taking place, the battle on the eastern front in the city of Stalingrad was also underway. This battle would also dramatically alter the course of the war. During the first five months of 1942, the Germans and Soviets recuperated from the horrific fighting of the previous winter. The Soviet Union was now the beneficiary of lend-lease aid from the United States and received food, locomotives, fuel, vehicles, and clothing. The Red Army offensives in the next years would have been impossible without American aid. Stalin reequipped his army and added more soldiers. The German army also used the winter to bring its army up to full strength. Nearly one-half million new

Soviet soldiers fought through thick smoke and dust left by a fierce German air attack on Stalingrad.

recruits were added to the German forces. By the spring thaw, the Germans still held an area of the Soviet Union roughly the size of the entire United States east of the Mississippi River.

The fighting on the eastern front would largely depend on the leadership abilities of the two opposing dictators, Adolf Hitler and Joseph Stalin. After the German failure to take Moscow, Hitler replaced thirty of his generals and named himself commander in chief. Stalin had acted as supreme commander of the Soviet forces since the beginning of the war. Both men exercised extraordinary control over the war, from grand strategy to day-to-day tactics. Hitler had an uncanny gift for innovative strategy. His daring plans often achieved tremendous surprise and success. Yet this flair was balanced by his tendency to improvise, his constant overruling of his generals, and his reckless squandering of German troops in desperate gambles. Stalin's interference with the day-to-day decisions of his generals also hampered the Red Army. The millions of Soviet prisoners and casualties during the start of Operation Barbarossa could be directly blamed on Stalin's unwillingness to heed the invasion warnings. Yet Stalin wisely resisted the reckless gambles that characterized Hitler's tactics. The Red Army always kept a sizable force in reserve to ensure it would be able to regroup no matter how devastating the defeat.

Hitler designed a plan for a new offensive for the spring of 1942. There would be no new attack on Moscow. The primary objective was to seize the southern part of the Soviet Union for its agricultural, industrial, and mineral wealth. Two separate army groups were assembled, containing almost half of all the German forces in the war. One army would march toward the city of Stalingrad, and the other would head southward to the oil-rich Caucasus region. The offensive began in June 1942. German troops advanced rapidly, destroying an entire Soviet army in the first

Street fighting was intense. Soviet soldiers took up positions in houses on the outskirts of Stalingrad.

two days. In the attack, 500,000 Soviet soldiers were taken prisoner. After several weeks, the Soviet army retreated to Stalingrad. Hitler's generals argued that the German army should move immediately to destroy the Soviet forces in Stalingrad. Hitler, however, considered the campaign to be as good as won. Repeating his error of the previous year, he diverted troops away from Stalingrad southward to assist in the fighting in the Caucasus. As a result, the advance on Stalingrad was fatally delayed for weeks. Hitler thus paved the way for Germany's eventual defeat in the war.

The Nightmare of Stalingrad

The city of Stalingrad had special emotional significance for Stalin. It had been renamed in his honor in 1928. (The city was renamed Volgograd after Stalin's death.) He ordered the city to be held at all costs. All of its citizens were mobilized. Every man and boy was enrolled in the army. The Soviet army was once again commanded by Zhukov, the hero of the Moscow defense. The assault would not be an easy one. The Volga River ran through the middle of Stalingrad. Unless the Germans were able to push across the river, the Red Army would be free to bombard the German troops with heavy artillery from the other side. Hitler committed the Sixth Army, led by Gen. Friedrich Paulus, along with the Fourth Panzer Army to the campaign.

The German assault began in late August. A fierce air attack left Stalingrad in flames. As fighting intensified, thick smoke and dust enveloped the city. One German officer wrote in his diary, "Stalingrad is no longer a town. By day, it is an enormous cloud of burning, blinding smoke. It is a vast furnace lit by the reflection of the flames." No previous battle was as horrible as this one. Each street, each building, each room was defended by the Soviet soldiers and citizens. The Germans used flamethrowers and grenades to root out the Soviets. But they did not leave. The Soviets set booby traps and mines in every building as they tried to outwit the Germans and save their city.

Fighting for a single factory or apartment building might rage for days. The top floors would be controlled by the Soviets, the ones below by the Germans. The stairways were no-man's-land. The Germans had to move room by room, floor by floor, until the entire building was captured. Once outnumbered, the Soviet soldiers escaped to a neighboring building by way of fire escapes and chimneys. Then, the fight for the new location would begin. The two sides fought this brutal, hand-to-hand combat for eighty days and eighty nights. It was a living nightmare for every soldier.

The biggest German advance came in mid-October. The Germans captured the gigantic Red October factory and seized

The Air War in Europe

One of the military campaigns that helped give World War II its distinctive character was the Allied air war against Nazi Germany from 1943 to 1945. The devastated cities of Europe became the symbols of the destructiveness of the war. Both the American and British air forces joined the air war, but they pursued entirely different strategies. The Americans emphasized daytime, precision bombing raids on key economic targets, such as arms factories, fuel depots, and railroads. The British endorsed a policy of nighttime "area bombing," involving the massive bombardment of entire German cities rather than specific targets.

The Americans believed that pinpoint attacks on critical targets would cripple the Nazis faster and more efficiently, while causing fewer civilian casualties, than area bombing. The American pilots were aided by an advanced bombsight that made accurate targeting possible. The bombsight was said to be so precise that a bombardier could "drop a bomb in a pickle barrel" from twenty thousand feet.

The American heavy bombers, the B-17 Flying Fortress and B-24 Liberator, flew in three squadrons of seven planes each. Their combat formation resembled a flying wedge, with the lead squadron in the middle and the others stacked to the right and left. It enabled the planes to coordinate their bombs and ward off enemy fighters. Each plane had a crew of ten, with pilots, bombardier, navigator, radar operator, and gunners. The pilots required nerves of steel. They had to hold their position steady as they came under fire by antiaircraft guns and Luftwaffe planes. It took great courage to hold on course toward the ground target as other American planes in the squadron were knocked out of the sky. By 1943, the chances of a pilot surviving his tour of duty of twenty-five missions was little better than one in three.

The American campaign from 1943 to 1944 paralyzed the German economy. It disrupted oil production so badly that barely a handful of Luftwaffe planes had enough fuel to get off the ground. It critically damaged rail transport

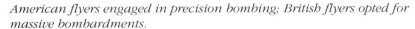

American flyers engaged in precision bombing; British flyers opted for massive bombardments.

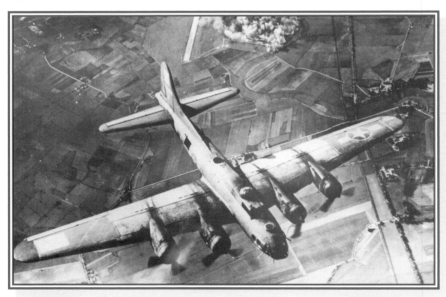

in France on the eve of the Allied invasion, which hampered German troop movements. And the campaign drained men from the regular German army. More than two million men and women, who might otherwise have served in combat at the front, were needed to operate the antiaircraft defenses.

Early on, the British had attempted precision bombing, but because of the notorious inaccuracy of its pilots—only one plane in ten delivered its bombs within five miles of the target—they switched to area bombing. Their strategy was to destroy the German people's will to fight. One of the first major raids in July 1943 on Hamburg provoked a horrifying fire storm. As fires in the center of the city spread, hot air rose and sucked in the surrounding air, feeding more fires. The fire storm created winds up to 150 miles per hour, the force of a hurricane. It uprooted trees and tossed cars into the air. Temperatures reached eighteen hundred degrees Fahrenheit. Asphalt streets were set on fire. Civilians who sought refuge in bomb shelters suffocated. Fifty thousand civilians were killed, and more than one million became refugees.

From mid-1943 through the spring of 1944, the British constantly attacked Berlin. The war had so far scarcely touched the capital. Its dance halls, restaurants, hotels, and theaters had flourished. The wave of bombing devastated the city. Although only 6000 people were killed—Berliners had built a vast system of deep underground shelters—1.5 million were left homeless. The worst British bombing of the war occurred in February 1945, when the RAF attacked the city of Dresden. The city was transformed into a blazing inferno, visible to airplanes almost two hundred miles away. The city had been jammed with refugees, so no one knows exactly how many people died in the raid, though estimates range as high as 300,000.

The costs of the area bombing campaign were tragically high. Millions of Germans were left homeless, 600,000 civilians were killed, and 800,000 were seriously injured. Children represented 20 percent of the casualties. The policy proved to be ineffective as well. It did not intimidate the population or weaken morale to the breaking point, nor did it seriously disrupt the economy. Most cities returned to normal less than a month after the bombings. Many people questioned the morality of the bombing campaign. Such random attacks on civilians seemed to make a mockery of the Allies' claim that they were fighting a "just war." Critics argued that this terror bombing of civilians should be outlawed as a war crime.

Nevertheless, the devastating loss of life as a result of the bombing illustrated an important point about the nature of war. At the beginning of every war, the generals who plan the fighting and the people on the home front have only the vaguest idea of the amount of suffering that will result. It is unimaginable that hundreds of thousands, even millions, could die in the course of a single battle or bombing raid. Yet what seems totally unbelievable at the start of a war may become commonplace policy by the end of it. In order to achieve a victory, both military leaders and the general public learn to accept and become accustomed to huge losses. This process helps explain why the Dresden bombings, the firebombing of Tokyo that left one million dead, and the atomic bomb attacks on Japan were not greeted with complete shock.

several ferry crossings. The Soviets were driven into a narrow pocket eight miles long and one mile deep against the Volga River. At some places, the Germans came as close as three hundred yards to the river. The Soviets had already lost 150,000 men, but they held on against all odds. Their motto was "There is no land beyond the Volga." Reinforcements, supplies, and wounded people were ferried back and forth across the river every night.

For the Germans, there seemed to be no end in sight to the stalemate. Hitler was obsessed with capturing the city. Stalingrad had become, in his mind, the ultimate test of will between the Germans and Soviets. He completely lost all sense of perspective of the battle. Even if his troops did push the Soviets over the Volga, it would be a minor accomplishment at a catastrophic cost. The German Sixth Army had already lost half its men. Most important, the Germans' northern and southern flanks were dangerously exposed. They were protected by underequipped armies from Germany's allies—Italy, Hungary, and Romania. There were simply not enough German units to fill the gap. If these flanks were overrun, the German forces at Stalingrad would be cut off. Hitler, as usual, underestimated the Red Army and believed he had already won the battle.

An Enormous Trap

Stalingrad, in reality, was the bait in a gigantic military trap. This had been the Soviet strategy from the start of the battle. The forces in the city were to hold fast, while reserves gathered in the north and southeast. The Soviets planned to encircle the German forces and destroy Paulus's army. By November, the Red Army had assembled more than one million men and nine hundred tanks. Their attack was launched on November 19. The Soviets crushed the armies guarding the German flanks. Within four days, the two detachments of the Soviet army met. The 250,000 men of the Sixth Army were completely surrounded.

Paulus signaled Hitler: "Army heading for disaster. It is essential to withdraw all divisions from Stalingrad." But Hitler refused to retreat from the Volga. He insisted the Luftwaffe could resupply the surrounded Sixth Army. This would enable the Germans to survive until other German forces broke through the Soviet encirclement. This plan, however, was pure fantasy. The daily supply requirements needed by the Germans were far beyond the capacity of the Luftwaffe to deliver. It would have required every airplane in the Luftwaffe, operating for an entire year, to supply Paulus's army. A German counterattack from the south came within thirty-five miles of the city on December 16, but Paulus made no attempt to break through the Soviet lines. He refused to move without the explicit order from Hitler, which never came.

The Sixth Army slowly disintegrated inside the city. Once the last airfield was seized by the Red Army, the Germans' food and ammunition supplies dropped drastically. The German troops were frostbitten, half-starving, and incapable of fighting. On January 8, the Soviets offered generous surrender terms, promising food and medical aid. But Paulus rejected the offer. Two days later, the Red Army began a ferocious bombardment of the city by seven thousand heavy artillery guns. It was the heaviest concentration of artillery fire in history. On January 30, 1943, Hitler promoted Paulus to field marshal. No German field marshal had ever surrendered or been captured. Hitler hoped that the honor would strengthen Paulus's resolve to either commit suicide or die fighting to the last gasp. After his headquarters was overrun on January 31, however, Paulus surrendered. Ninety thousand Germans were taken prisoner, along with twenty thousand wounded. Upon news of the German surrender, the bells of the Kremlin rang through the streets of Moscow.

Stalingrad was the first decisive Soviet victory of the war. It was achieved at a frightful cost. The entire city lay in ruins. During the battles, 750,000 Soviets, 300,000 Germans, and 450,000 German allies were killed. Alongside the victory at Alamein, and the American triumphs at Midway and Guadalcanal in the Pacific, the battle for Stalingrad transformed the course of the war. The German army never recovered from the fighting. "The God of war," Hitler told his chief of staff, "has gone over to the other side." A long struggle lay ahead, but for the first time, a victory for the Allies seemed a real possibility.

Unconditional Surrender

A meeting between Roosevelt and Churchill at Casablanca, in Morocco, on January 14, 1943, reflected the feeling that the Allies were winning. It was at this conference that Roosevelt stated that the Allies would fight for an "unconditional surrender" from Germany. Although Roosevelt later insisted the phrase was merely a harmless, off-the-cuff remark to reporters, it was a masterstroke of political rhetoric. The very phrase itself highlighted a fundamental fact about the war—Germany was now losing. There would be no turning back. The British and Soviets had dealt Nazi Germany staggering defeats. Now, it was up to the United States to deliver the knockout blow.

CHAPTER FOUR

The Americans Take Command

B y 1943, the Allies were clearly in a position to triumph over Germany. It was the Americans' time to shine. The overwhelming economic and military might of the United States would dominate the remainder of the war. It would be the American factories that produced the countless jeeps, planes, tanks, trucks, and ammunition that fueled the Allied armies. It would be the American army that launched the major offensives in 1943 and 1944 in North Africa, Italy, and France. Although there was still a long way to go before the Nazis were defeated, it was the American soldiers who would deliver the final blow to them.

The American soldiers were known as GIs (an abbreviation taken from the phrase "government issue"), dogfaces, or foot soldiers. Most were in their early twenties. Few of the troops or their officers had ever seen combat before. Still, no amount of training could have prepared them for the harsh reality of their first battles. Combat has a distinctive sound: the whistle of artillery shells passing overhead, the hum of the dive-bombers, the rumble of approaching tanks, and the ping of rifle fire. There was nothing quite as horrifying as the ordeal of an artillery bombardment. Soldiers would close their eyes, and even the most seasoned veterans would grow weak at the sound of shells landing nearby. Every muscle of a soldier's body would tense with the expectation that the next shell would be the one that gets him.

The inexperienced American troops on the front line had to quickly overcome their normal instincts and inhibitions. They learned to stand and hold their ground in the face of a frontal attack or heavy fire. They learned to abandon the relative safety

The Life of GI Joe

Combat troops served on the front lines twenty-four hours a day, seven days a week, for months on end. If they were lucky, these soldiers might get a leave once a month. During World War II, American soldiers were rarely pulled off their frontline duty unless they were wounded. Men served in combat for years without ever going home. The most experienced American troops went from one campaign to another, without a break. Veterans of the First Infantry Division, known as the Big Red One because of their sleeve patch with a red numeral one, were involved in the landings in North Africa, Sicily, Italy, and Normandy.

Combat soldiers lived in a small, self-contained world. They knew nothing of, and cared little for, grand strategy. Their view of the war extended no further than their own platoon or regiment. They learned not to look beyond the next battlefield. One veteran admitted: "I didn't think the war was ever going to end. I thought that for the rest of our lives, we should be fighting one way or another."

Life in combat meant digging trenches every single day. It meant endless marches, dragging one foot in front of the other mile after mile, all the while staring at the back of the soldier in front. It meant worrying constantly about getting killed or wounded. It meant a deep weariness that never seemed to go away. Even the infrequent rest breaks never lasted more than a few hours. After months of this ordeal, bright-eyed, fresh-faced twenty-year-olds began to look like old men. American soldiers, wrote the author and cartoonist Bill Mauldin, ended up with a peculiar look:

> A soldier who has been a long time in the line does have a "look" in his eyes that anyone with practice can discern. It's a look of dullness, eyes that look without seeing, eyes that see without transferring any response to the mind. It's a look that is the display room for the thoughts that lie behind it—exhaustion, lack of sleep, tension for too long, weariness that is too great, fear beyond fear, misery to the point of numbness, a look of surpassing indifference to anything anybody can do to you. It's a look I dread to see of men.

The war was indeed a testament to the resilience of the human body and spirit. Even after the terror of battle, soldiers would still perk up to listen to a wisecrack or joke, even though these tended to be morbid. In one classic joke of the war, a pilot was shot down and crashed in a tree. When a group of soldiers reached him, they found the pilot's legs were trapped beneath the wreckage, his arms were twisted at a grotesque angle, his chest was crushed, and his face was a bloody mess. When the pilot was finally taken out of the plane, a medic asked him how he felt. The pilot smiled and said, "It only hurts when I laugh."

Humor was an ever-present feature of a GI's life. A graffiti drawing with the caption "Kilroy Was Here" was marked on buildings, latrines, and walls across Europe. The picture was of a long, pathetic nose hanging over a wall with two large eyes. No one had any idea who first did the drawing, but every GI understood the message. If something bad happened, "Kilroy" was automatically to blame. And for thousands of GIs in Italy, Bill Mauldin's cartoons in the army newspaper *Stars and Stripes* helped put smiles on their faces. His main characters were Willie and Joe, unshaven, grimy dogfaces fighting in the Italian mountains. They griped about the weather, the food, and the "rear echelon heroes." These were the soldiers or officers who were fortunate enough to spend the entire war behind the lines in comfortable posts. (Of the millions of American troops who served in the war, only a very small percentage ever saw actual combat duty.) Mauldin's characters became the champion of the enlisted man. In one cartoon, Willie told Joe: "Yesterday, ya saved my life an' I swore I'd pay ya back. Here's my last pair of clean socks."

American troops storm the North African coast in their first real test of battle.

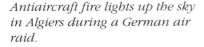

Antiaircraft fire lights up the sky in Algiers during a German air raid.

of their trenches and move forward on the attack. Every soldier could relate a story of a close call in combat. For example, one officer was leading a platoon at night, with his men behind him walking in single file. Suddenly, a mine went off, killing his entire platoon. The officer had miraculously walked through a mine field unharmed. Another soldier reported that a bullet passed clean through his helmet across the top of his head. His hair and scalp were scorched, but otherwise he escaped without injury.

Conditions in the American army were anything but ideal. Each man carried his own food on his back. Canned rations, called C rations, consisted of a hard biscuit, cold stew, beans, Spam, dehydrated potatoes, and if a soldier was lucky, canned peaches. Physical discomfort was an everyday fact of life. The men slept on bedrolls on the hard ground. They had no hot water, hot meals, milk, or newspapers. The most valuable commodity in the army was toilet paper. The soldiers never took off their clothes except for their shoes, and they had the luxury of a cold bath once a month. The men went days without sleep and were constantly exhausted. A soldier would close his eyes for a brief moment and be fast asleep within seconds. These infantrymen were the heart and soul of the American army. American reporter Ernie Pyle said: "I love the infantry because they are the underdogs. They are the mud-rain-frost-and-wind guys. They have no comforts and they learn to live without the necessities. And in the end, they are the guys that wars can't be won without."

The first test of battle for the American army came in North Africa in 1943. Some American generals favored opening up an immediate second front in France in 1943. But the American army was just getting up to full fighting strength and was not ready to embark on a full-scale invasion involving millions of

men. Instead, Roosevelt and the Allies settled on a smaller campaign in North Africa that would give the untested American troops valuable combat experience.

The Americans in North Africa

American and British troops landed in Morocco and Algeria four days after the victory at Alamein. It was the largest invasion using coordinated land and sea troops in history, with five hundred ships carrying 100,000 men. Commander in chief of this Operation Torch was Lt. Gen. Dwight D. Eisenhower, who was nicknamed Ike. The initial fighting against French troops loyal to the pro-German Petain regime resulted in a quick defeat by the Americans who suffered only minor casualties. This first taste of the war left the American troops in a cocky mood. Many soldiers assumed that the war was as good as won now that the United States was in it. The Americans, however, had not yet encountered the battle-hardened German army.

A short time after the Allied landings, Hitler shifted the Fifth Panzer Army to Tunisia to fight the Americans. Tunisia is a mountainous country, with steep ridges and narrow passes connecting to flat desert valleys. One of the first American attacks on the German lines came on January 21, 1943. German troops secured positions on both sides of a narrow pass. Their tanks, machine guns, and antitank guns were dug in along the ridge. The American troops came in from west to east, which meant the bright midday sun shone directly in their eyes. They stumbled completely unawares into the German forces, who opened fire. German dive-bombers stormed the trapped soldiers and tanks. The American troops retreated with heavy losses in men and equipment.

A German assault in February drove hard into the American forces. The subsequent battle at Kasserine Pass became one of the worst moments in American military history. On February 19, German panzer units outflanked the American troops making their way through the narrow pass. German soldiers ended up behind the American lines and launched a ferocious attack against the unsuspecting troops. The American soldiers panicked under fire and retreated in total disarray. Platoons broke off into individual units. Soldiers grabbed the nearest vehicle and fled as fast as possible. A complete rout was avoided only because a British armored division filled the gap left by the disoriented U.S. troops. The American army had three hundred dead, three thousand wounded, and three thousand captured in the battle.

After the horrible defeat at Kasserine Pass, the command of the American forces was given to Gen. George S. Patton. Patton was one of the most colorful American generals, known for the pearl-handled revolvers he wore as side arms. He was also the

Gen. Dwight D. Eisenhower (below, seated on the left) led the largest land-sea invasion the world had ever seen. Gen. George S. Patton, pictured in lower photograph, was a brilliant military tactician.

Thousands of spent German shells lie in piles in front of a damaged building in Bizerte, Tunisia (left). A German rowboat and rifle on the Tunisian coast (right) provide reminders of the German presence in North Africa.

Americans' best tactician, and his gung ho leadership was bound to shake up the American ranks. He instituted regular drills and a rigid dress code to instill some needed discipline in the ragged American troops. In addition, Patton's tactical brilliance helped the Americans achieve victory on the battlefield. Largely due to his generalship, the American army scored several successes against the Germans, driving them into a smaller and smaller pocket around Tunis, the capital of Tunisia.

By May, the Germans were hopelessly trapped by Patton's forces in the west and Montgomery's army from the east. Rommel went to Germany to plead with Hitler to withdraw the German forces from North Africa. Hitler's reaction was predictable. He removed Rommel from command and ordered his soldiers to fight to "the last bullet." But on May 13, 1943, the 250,000 German soldiers in Tunisia surrendered.

The North African campaign was an important first test for the Americans. And their taste of success was something to be savored. The feeling of exultation after a victory in combat was unequalled. "Winning a battle," wrote Ernie Pyle, "is like winning at poker or catching lots of fish." The common experience of battle drew the soldiers closer to each other. They developed a common bond that proved an invaluable aid in the next round of fighting.

With the campaign in North Africa successfully concluded, there was considerable debate about where the next American assault should be directed. The head of the Joint Chiefs of Staff, Gen. George Marshall, pressed for an invasion of France. But, a critical shortage of landing craft—most of which were committed to the American navy in the Pacific—convinced President Roosevelt to agree to an invasion of Italy instead. The hope was that the Allied campaign would drive the Italian government out of the war and also trap a large number of German divisions that might otherwise be used as reinforcements on the eastern front. The primary Allied objective was to capture Rome. It would be an important psychological and political victory for the Allies before the invasion of France took place.

The Italian Campaign

On July 10, 1943, 150,000 American and British forces landed in Sicily. After putting up a stiff resistance, the Germans evacuated the island on August 11. The Allied forces failed to inflict much damage on the German army, but the invasion did have a major impact on Italian politics. The Italian people had grown weary of war and two decades of Benito Mussolini's fascist rule. Protests had erupted earlier in the year in northern factories, and an underground resistance movement had formed. With the American invasion, the time was ripe for the overthrow of Mussolini. Members of the fascist cabinet had Mussolini arrested and imprisoned. The new government negotiated with the Allies and signed a peace treaty on September 3.

Italians danced happily in the streets upon hearing of the armistice, but their celebration was premature. Within hours, the Germans rushed troops into Rome and occupied northern and central Italy. They disarmed the Italian army, arrested Allied sympathizers, and chased the new Italian leaders into exile. The German army, under the command of Field Marshal Albert Kesselring, established a defensive line below Rome to meet the Allied threat. On September 6, German paratroopers performed a daring mission, rescuing Mussolini from the mountain resort where he was imprisoned. Mussolini was named head of a tiny fascist state, Salo, in northern Italy. He remained there until April 1945, when he was captured and executed by the Italian resistance movement.

Tanks await transport from a French naval base in Tunisia two days before the Allied invasion of Sicily. The Germans put up a stiff resistance, but evacuated Sicily after one month.

The Italian Campaign

AUSTRIA

HUNGARY

SWITZERLAND

Rapido River

MONTE CASSINO

CASSINO

36th Infantry Division Advances

SCALE OF MILES
0   1

YUGOSLAVIA

Pisa

ITALY

ADRIATIC SEA

Corsica

1944

Rome

Allies enter Rome June 4, 1944

Anzio

Cassino

1943

Naples

Salerno

ALBANIA

1943

TYRRHENIAN SEA

Sardinia

1943

MEDITERRANEAN SEA

Allied Drives

Messina

SICILY 1943

MEDITERRANEAN SEA

SCALE OF MILES
0   50   100   150   200

TUNISIA

A medic gives blood plasma to an American soldier wounded by shrapnel in Sicily.

On September 2, 1943, at 3:30 in the morning, seventy thousand men of the American Fifth Army commanded by Gen. Mark Clark, landed at Salerno, 120 miles south of Rome. British forces simultaneously crossed the Strait of Messina from Sicily to Reggio di Calabria at the base of Italy. The Americans hoped to be in Naples, thirty miles away, within five days, but it would be tough going. Because the American landing craft had been spotted offshore by German planes, there was no hope of a surprise landing. Yet General Clark mistakenly believed the element of surprise could still be achieved if his troops landed without the customary bombardment of the beach by navy ships. The Germans, however, were not fooled. Because they did not have to defend against the American navy's guns, the Germans were able to put up a furious fight. It was not until nightfall that the Americans were able to push their way four miles inland.

By the end of the second day, the Americans still had only a precarious hold on the beach. The Germans quickly called up two seasoned divisions and launched a counterattack. Their tanks overran one battalion and at one point pushed within two

miles of the beachhead, the area on the beach that had been secured by the invading American troops. Only a handful of American infantrymen and two artillery units stood in their path. American officers on the scene hastily improvised a new defensive line. They requisitioned clerks, cooks, drivers, and mechanics from headquarters and placed them on the front lines. When the Germans renewed their assault, the American artillery brigades opened fire continually on the attackers. The makeshift infantry stood its ground, and the Americans narrowly averted a total disaster.

Two days later, the Eighty-second Airborne Division dropped thirteen hundred men inside the embattled American lines. Two other units of reinforcements landed by sea. The navy moved its destroyers close to shore and pounded the German lines with nonstop shelling. The Germans were slowly pushed back into the hills. Yet it was not until late September that the American troops finally broke free of the hills around Salerno, and not until October 5 that Naples was liberated. Twelve thousand men were killed in Salerno, the heaviest losses to date by the American army in the war.

An American cargo ship hit by a German bomb explodes off the coast of Sicily (left). An American soldier stands before an altar in a damaged Catholic church in Italy (right) as sunlight streams through the shattered ceiling.

The March Toward Rome

Once past Naples, the Americans began the long journey toward Rome, which they hoped to seize within six to eight weeks. However, it would be ten months before they reached their goal. To get to Rome, the American troops had to pass through treacherous mountain terrain that concealed hidden dangers and a wealth of military obstacles. A mountain range, the Apennines, runs down the center of Italy. A series of ridges extends east and west to the coasts, and between the ridges lay deep valleys and rivers. The rivers, ridges, and mountains offered a succession of defensive strongholds for the Germans. There were only a few roads, and these were vulnerable to German attack from the hills. The countryside was impassable to tanks and other vehicles.

The fighting in the Italian campaign was the bloodiest, most grueling confrontation that American soldiers had with the Germans during the war. Italy's mountainsides became the site of bitter, small-scale fighting. Each German stronghold had to be captured in combat at close quarters. The steep hills were filled with booby traps and mines. The Germans strung thin trip wires, fixed to a grenade, across hill trails, in abandoned houses, and near latrines. As the campaign stretched into the winter, the freezing cold, rain, and icy winds made each soldier's life miserable. They trudged knee-deep in mud for months. There never seemed to be an end in sight to the fighting. For every hill that the Americans captured, there was always another one just like it up ahead. The psychological wear and tear on the troops was extreme.

Italians Embrace Americans

The one bit of encouragement for the American GIs was the warm reception they received from the Italian people. Most Italians regarded the American troops as liberators rather than the enemy. The brutal Nazi occupation and the hardships of war had become so intolerable that most Italians could not wait for the Americans to arrive. They waved American flags, gave the soldiers wine, fruit, and cheese, and helped them pinpoint German troop positions and movements. Because so many of their fellow citizens had journeyed to the United States before the war as immigrants, the Italians felt a special bond with the American soldiers. Ernie Pyle wrote: "In the very remotest and most ancient towns, we found that half the people had relatives in America and there was always somebody popping up from behind every bush or around every corner who had lived twelve years in Buffalo or thirty years in Chicago."

It took three months of hard fighting before the American forces reached the outskirts of the Liri Valley. This was where the Americans hoped to begin their final push to Rome. The entrance to the valley, however, was guarded by two natural obstacles: the swiftly flowing Rapido River and the imposing peak called Monte Cassino, which rose seventeen hundred feet above the town of Cassino. Atop Monte Cassino was a medieval abbey that had once been captured in 1799 by the young Napoleon. Now, it was the linchpin of the German defense and contained one of the best German divisions. Before they could reach Rome, the Allies would have to overcome these barriers.

The crossing of the Rapido River was the first operation mounted by the Americans. A river crossing is one of the most hazardous tasks an infantry unit has to perform, and this one was especially difficult. The river was only twenty-five feet wide, but its waters were ice-cold, ten feet deep, with dangerous rapids. The Germans placed booby traps and mines everywhere and set up machine guns and mortars or cannons, on the bluffs overlooking the water. They chopped down the trees on both riverbanks, eliminating any cover for the Americans. Because any daytime attack would provoke a hailstorm of fire, the river crossing had to be made at night, which was always dangerous.

The commanding officer of the thirty-sixth Infantry Division, the American unit assigned to the assault, feared that his troops would be slaughtered in the attack. He urged headquarters to reconsider but was ordered by General Clark to proceed as planned. Soldiers in the division knew full well what kind of horrors awaited them. "We had the feeling we were being sacrificed," one soldier confessed, "a feeling that we couldn't win, but we'd give it our damnedest."

An Unforgivable Maneuver

On January 20, 1944, at 8:00 P.M., three thousand soldiers moved forward, carrying rubber rafts and wooden boats. When they reached within one mile of the river, German mortar shells began to land among the American ranks. By the time they reached the river, one-third of their boats were destroyed. Numerous soldiers accidentally walked into the mine fields. Fewer than one thousand men managed to get across the river. They dug in and waited for reinforcements, but only a few hundred more succeeded in crossing. By dawn, the German shelling increased, sinking other craft attempting to cross. The small American foothold on the German side came under heavy attack

A 240-mm howitzer is readied to fire into German-held territory near Mignano, Italy, in January 1944 (left). U.S. troops fire a 155-mm gun, known as a "Long Tom," near Nettuno, Italy (right).

by tanks, artillery, and mortar fire. By mid-morning, the Americans were forced to withdraw across the Rapido.

In the afternoon, they tried once again to break through the German defenses. More and more boats were hit. The American GIs were tossed overboard, and many drowned. The soldiers' bodies began to pile up on the far bank. By the end of the second day, the Americans completely stopped the attack. Every American soldier who had reached the German side of the Rapido had either been killed, wounded, or captured. The German line had not budged an inch. A few months later, the Americans crossed the river at a more favorable location. The bitter American soldiers who participated in the Rapido River fiasco never forgave General Clark for ordering the suicidal operation.

The Americans then turned to Monte Cassino. The first joint American-British attack in late January managed to get within four hundred yards of the monastery before they were stopped. Heavy shelling from the Germans on top of the summit forced the Allied troops to retreat even farther. An American soldier, Harold Bond, recalled the horror of the bombardment in his memoir, *Return to Cassino:*

> The air was filled with sounds as if every gun in the valley had found us at the same time. We pushed down as far as we could in terror, and the ground all around us shook with gigantic explosions. Huge showers of earth rained down on top of our heads. The air was full of flying dirt and shrapnel. In such a shelling as this, each man is isolated from everyone else. Death is immediately in front of them. He only knows that his legs and arms are still there and that he has not been hit yet. In the next instant he might.

On three separate occasions from February to April, the Allies assaulted the stronghold but were turned away. The

Ernie Pyle: War Correspondent

War correspondents brought the sights, sounds, and feel of the war into millions of American homes. The best reporters traveled with the frontline troops, sharing the same discomforts and facing the same dangers.

Ernie Pyle is generally regarded as the most famous reporter of World War II. His column was syndicated in almost three hundred newspapers in the United States. At his peak, Pyle had a daily readership of sixty million people. He won a Pulitzer Prize in 1943 for his distinguished reporting.

Pyle covered the campaigns in North Africa, Sicily, Italy, France, and the Pacific. He was the GIs' best friend, with a special fondness for the infantrymen. He wrote about the food they ate, the clothes they wore, and their aching muscles and weariness. For Pyle, the infantrymen were the sort of men who never saw themselves as heroes yet exhibited quiet courage and dignity in the face of grave danger. Pyle gave Americans a vivid, realistic portrait of the war, stripped of the glamour and romanticism found in the movies and magazines. He wrote:

In the magazines, war seemed romantic and exciting, full of heroes and vitality…certainly there were great tragedies, unbelievable heroism…but when I sat down to write, I saw instead men…suffering and wishing they were somewhere else…all of them desperately hungry for somebody to talk to other than themselves, no women to be heroes in front of, damned little wine to drink, precious little song, cold and fairly dirty, just toiling from day to day in a world full of insecurity, discomforts, homesickness and a dulled sense of danger.

Pyle narrowly escaped death on several occasions. At Anzio, he was almost killed when an artillery shell struck the house where he was sleeping. During the Normandy campaign, he was traveling with an American unit that was mistakenly bombed by its own planes. In April 1945, Pyle's luck ran out. He was killed by a Japanese sniper on the tiny island of Ie Jima, west of Okinawa. He was forty-four years old.

Reporter Ernie Pyle wrote vivid and realistic accounts of the lives of infantrymen at war. He wrote of hungry soldiers lining up for food and of lonely, tired soldiers who longed for home.

second attack was preceded by a devastating bombardment by 135 planes that reduced the monastery to rubble. Yet it failed to dislodge the German soldiers. They occupied the huge craters and deep cellars created by the bombing, making it an even more formidable obstacle. Fifteen thousand Allied troops were killed in the attempts to overtake it.

With the Allied offensives stalled, the Allied command decided to try to take Rome. They planned a surprise amphibious landing, or a combined land and sea attack, behind the German lines at the port of Anzio, thirty-five miles south of Rome. The American troops would make a swift thrust toward the capital, thereby threatening the German forces anchored at Monte Cassino with an attack from the rear. The Germans would have no alternative but to retreat to the north of Rome. The landing on January 22, 1944, was unopposed, and the Americans achieved total surprise. The first units ashore encountered only sporadic German resistance. By midday, the American forces had advanced three miles and put all their troops safely ashore. The American commander, Gen. John Lucas, however, was a cautious tactician and he failed to fully use his advantage. Instead of driving inland immediately to cut off the German supply routes, he halted his troops and waited more than a week while more and more American soldiers and supplies poured onshore.

It was only on the ninth day that Lucas finally ordered his troops to begin an attack, which quickly failed. By this time, the Germans had mobilized emergency forces and had more than forty thousand troops in the area. On the next day, the Germans counterattacked and came close to driving the Americans into the sea. The Americans were forced onto a tiny beachhead, every inch of which was within range of German artillery. For four months, the American troops were pinned down by continual artillery fire from the hills overlooking the town. The beachhead was nicknamed "hell's half acre" by the GIs. Repeated attempts to break out of the encirclement failed. Anzio was widely regarded among American soldiers as a symbol of the worst kind of military disaster.

By May 1944, none of the Allied plans were progressing. Their armies had advanced only seventy miles in eight months. In mid-May, the Allied forces launched a final offensive to crack the German lines. In the south below Cassino, French troops, led by Moroccan tribesmen with special mountain-climbing skills, made their way through mountainous terrain that the Germans regarded as impassable. The French then moved west, threatening the German flanks. Fifty thousand men of the Polish army stormed Monte Cassino and captured the fortress after six days of brutal fighting. At the same time, the American forces at Anzio finally broke through the German lines. These Allied successes placed the German army in peril of encirclement. The Germans retreated to a new defensive line near Pisa in the north.

General Clark chose not to cut the German army off and instead moved his forces toward Rome, which the Germans had left unguarded. On June 4, 1944, the American army made a triumphant entry into Rome to the cheers of ecstatic Italians. Thousands of soldiers poured into the city and spent the night camping out in Rome's streets, sidewalks, cafes, and monuments. One Roman woman remembered the amazing transformation: "The next morning, the air, the smell of Rome had changed. Before, Rome had always smelled of cooking, wine, dried fish and garlic. Now suddenly it was Chesterfields [cigarettes]." The capture of Rome was the psychological victory the Allies needed before they invaded France.

The Invasion of France

The Allied preparations for the long-awaited invasion of France had begun in early 1943. At the Casablanca conference, the Allies had agreed that an invasion of northern France—code-named Overlord—should take place no later than May 1944. General Eisenhower was named Supreme Allied Commander of Operation Overlord. He had risen from colonel to general in only three years with little combat experience. Many wondered how he would be able to command his more experienced colleagues. Despite his lack of tactical expertise, Eisenhower was a brilliant strategist and an unmatched administrator. His great talent was his ability to use the diverse personalities of his multinational staff efficiently and effectively.

Allied flights over France had provided detailed maps and photos of every inch of the French coastline. The choice of where to direct the invasion eventually came down to two alternatives: the Calais Peninsula or Normandy. Calais made military sense. Only twenty-two miles across the English Channel, it would make the quickest crossing and the road to Germany would be that much shorter. But the Germans had concentrated their strongest defenses in that region. Normandy, located between the Seine River and Cotentin Peninsula in northwest France, was a longer trip across the channel, but its beaches and tides were more favorable for a landing. After some deliberation, the Allies chose Normandy as the site of the invasion.

The plan for Operation Overload was to land two American divisions at beaches code-named Omaha and Utah, with two British and one Canadian divisions landing sixteen miles to the east at Juno, Sword, and Gold beaches. Airborne troops would secure the Allied flanks and seize bridges inland to prevent German reinforcements from reaching the beaches. After the beachhead was secured, the Allies planned to eventually bring ashore an additional one hundred divisions and begin the drive to Berlin.

Great Britain was totally overwhelmed with soldiers and equipment for the Normandy invasion. Since 1943, nearly one million Americans had passed through the country. The whole of southern England was covered with tanks, airplanes, jeeps, and row after row of army barracks. The British joked that their island was about to sink under the weight of all the Americans. Not every British citizen was overjoyed by the presence of so many Yanks, as they called American soldiers. Americans seemed to be in all their restaurants, movie theaters, and nightclubs and were dating most of the unattached British women. As one Londoner complained: "The Americans are overfed, overheight, oversexed—and over here."

Still, together the British and Americans anxiously awaited the launching of the invasion. Many regarded it as more than just another military operation. Eisenhower compared it to a "great crusade" that would put an end to the evil Nazi empire.

CHAPTER FIVE

Home Front

World War II profoundly affected every aspect of American society. It transformed the American economy and made the United States the greatest industrial and military power in the world. It produced the largest migration of Americans to other regions of the nation. It overturned the traditional role of American women. It marked an important first step in the transformation of American race relations. World War II remains perhaps the single most important event in American history in the twentieth century.

In 1940, the country still had not fully recovered from the Great Depression that started in 1929. The economy was sluggish, and the threat of unemployment still loomed. Memories of those difficult years lingered in American minds. Many were convinced that things were never going to improve. The war changed all that. After Pearl Harbor, the federal government launched a massive spending campaign to convert the nation to a full-time war economy. The resources of the entire country were mobilized for the war effort. The federal budget increased dramatically from $9 billion in 1939 to $100 billion in 1945. The government pumped money into the economy at the rate of $2.3 billion a month and businesses were given tax incentives and loans.

Factories everywhere were converted over to war production. Gigantic new plants were constructed in rolling farmlands, uninhabited deserts, and in the nation's cities. By 1944, 40 percent of the nation's economy was devoted to war production. Between 1941 and 1945, the "arsenal of democracy" built more

After Pearl Harbor, the nation converted to a full-time war economy. Here, aviation machinists work on an aircraft engine in Chicago.

Workers wipe down transparent noses for A-20 attack bombers at Douglas Aircraft plant in Long Beach, California (left) and a mechanic completes work on a rebuilt Wright Whirlwind airplane motor at a naval air base (right).

than 300,000 aircraft, 102,000 tanks, 37,000 warships, 372,000 artillery pieces, and 45 million tons of ammunition. Willow Run, an aircraft plant outside of Detroit, was the largest factory in the world. It turned out one B-24 Liberator bomber every sixty-three minutes. West Coast shipyards launched two ships a day. This feat of production was so impressive that Stalin, at an Allied conference, offered a toast: "To American production, without which this war would have been lost."

The American economy was not only larger but more efficient than that of any of its allies or enemies. American businesses successfully adopted assembly-line techniques to manufacture war materials. The production process was so efficient that any worker could be quickly trained and placed in an assembly line. American efficiency was also a direct result of the hard toil of its workers. During the war, Americans worked an average of six days, or fifty hours, a week. Union leaders agreed to a no-strike pledge in 1941, and only a small number of workers went out on strike.

The workers' patriotism was also an important factor. The men and women in the factories realized that the lives of American soldiers depended on their skill. They felt a personal need to push themselves to the limit and to make certain that the weapons they turned out would not fail in battle. As Ronald Bailey in *Homefront USA* describes:

For workers with ties to the battlefront—the fathers, mothers, brothers, sisters and wives on the production lines at home—there was a special incentive that outweighed everything else: the possibility that their own handiwork might somehow directly affect the life of a loved one. They relished the story of a seaman named Elgin Staples, whose ship went

down off Guadalcanal. Staples was swept over the side, but he survived thanks to a lifebelt, that proved, on later examination, to have been inspected, packed and stamped back home in Akron, Ohio, by his own mother.

The expanded economy brought renewed prosperity for most Americans. Wages and salaries went up, and people had much more money to spend. It was also a tremendous period of opportunity. Americans during the war moved more often, in greater numbers and over greater distances than ever before. Families from the East moved to cities in the Southwest and West to work in new defense factories located there. Almost 5.5 million people left their farms during the war to live and work in the defense centers. Wives followed their husbands to army bases around the country. As many as 20 million Americans—almost 15 percent of the population—moved during the war.

There were long lines in every bus and train station. City streets were packed with newcomers. Novelist John Dos Passos traveled around the country during wartime, and his words capture the hustle and bustle of the era:

> Once I was westbound from St. Paul, in fact it seemed as if EVERYONE was westbound. With the hum and rhythm of the bus, there was an undertone of talk—words—Seattle—Portland—San Francisco—Seattle—shipyards—Vancouver—how about housing—do you know anyone there? I have a cousin in Olympia—we'll go there first—then we can look around in Tacoma and Seattle. It wouldn't take any imagination at all to think that you were going west on a covered wagon and were a pioneer again.

These hectic travels altered the life of many Americans. People who had never left their small town or farm were now thrown together with people from different economic classes, ethnic backgrounds, and religions.

Women in the War Effort

As a result of the new economic opportunities, the role of women in American society was greatly transformed. Before the war, women represented 25 percent of the labor force; by 1944, they constituted 36 percent. Wartime labor shortages opened up thousands of jobs that had previously been held only by men. Many war plants actively recruited women. One firm advertised its openings with the slogan: "If you can drive a car, you can run a machine." Women of all ages and social backgrounds entered the work force. They took jobs as truck drivers, mechanics, crane operators, and welders. They pumped gas,

Women entered the work force in unprecedented numbers during the war. At top, a riveter takes a break from her work at the Lockheed Aircraft plant in Burbank, California. Above, a woman worker dons protective gear before cleaning the tops of blast furnaces at U.S. Steel Works in Gary, Indiana.

Hollywood Goes to War

Even before the United States entered the war, Hollywood was already producing movies sympathetic to the Allied cause. These films left no doubt that Hitler was bent on world domination and that the Nazis were undermining democracy at home. In *Confessions of a Nazi Spy,* for example, an FBI agent, played by Edward G. Robinson, hunts down Nazi spies.

War themes dominated many of the most popular movies of the period. In the bittersweet romance *Casablanca,* a nightclub owner, played by Humphrey Bogart, sacrifices his own happiness to save the resistance leader whose wife he loved. *Mrs. Miniver,* starring Greer Garson and Walter Pidgeon, shows an average British family living graciously and courageously under the constant strain of war.

The federal government took an active role in molding the types of films that were produced during the war. The Bureau of Motion Pictures met with Hollywood executives and urged filmmakers to make entertaining films that also contained a message. Movies, they argued, should show wounded men but should not alarm the public with combat scenes that are too violent or bloody. The democratic nature of the American cause should be emphasized by highlighting racially and ethnically mixed battalions. Every filmmaker should ask one question: "Will this picture help win the war?"

God Is My Co-Pilot, They Were Expendable, Thirty Seconds over Tokyo, and *Guadalcanal Diary* were just a few of the many combat epics that were produced during the 1940s. Many films showed American soldiers winning battles single-handedly, as actor Errol Flynn did in *Objective Burma.* Other films depicted dramatic last stands, where American soldiers went down in a defiant blaze of gunfire. Robert Taylor, starring in *Bataan,* vowed in his last moments: "It doesn't matter where a man dies, so long as he dies for freedom." Most war films distorted and glorified what actual fighting was like. "They didn't understand anything about the war. And they didn't try to understand," wrote the novelist James Jones. "Instead of showing the distressing complexity and puzzling diffusion of war, they pulled everything down to the level of good guy against bad guy." Perhaps the two most realistic portrayals were *The Story of GI Joe,* based on Ernie Pyle's reports, and *The Best Years of Our Lives,* which showed the problems veterans faced upon returning home.

War themes dominated many popular movies during World War II. Confessions of a Nazi Spy *told the tale of an FBI agent who hunts down Nazi spies.*

stoked steel, and operated drills. They secured professional positions at newspapers, universities, and law firms.

Of course, working women continued to perform all of their traditional duties at home. After a tiring ten-hour shift, a woman still had the household chores—washing, cooking, cleaning, and shopping—to do. There were few day-care centers in the United States, so working women had to find a neighbor or relative to watch their children. Women encountered frequent sexism on and off the job. They were generally paid lower wages than men for the same work. They were often insulted, harassed, and intimidated in the workplace. Men accused women workers of neglecting their children or of being less than "feminine" for wearing pants at work.

Despite the harassment, women thrived during the war. It was the first time many had ever earned a paycheck. Women enjoyed spending or saving the money they received. They gained self-confidence from their economic independence and from learning new skills. Rachel Wray recalled her own experience: "I remember my brother, who was in the air force at the time, and his friends laughed at me one day, thinking I couldn't learn this mechanical stuff. I can still see them, but it only made me more determined. I think it probably hurt their pride a little bit that I was capable of a job like this."

Of course, the war dramatically affected the lives of every American, not just women. In September 1940, the draft was reinstated. All males between the ages of eighteen and thirty-five were required to register with the local army board so that they could be called upon for military service if needed. In all, more than thirty-one million men registered for the draft. After Pearl Harbor, army and navy recruiting stations were overwhelmed with volunteers. Movie stars such as Henry Fonda, Clark Gable, and Jimmy Stewart enlisted, and so did sports heroes Ted Williams, Joe DiMaggio, and Joe Louis. Sixteen million men and women (in the noncombat Women Army Corps)—one of every eleven Americans—served in the armed forces.

Working women stuck with their jobs despite lower wages and frequent harassment from male coworkers.

"This Is the Army Mr. Jones"

Army recruits spent months in training camps, most of which were located in the South. Upon arrival, they were given drab, ill-fitting uniforms and quarter-inch crew cuts. They woke up at the crack of dawn for morning calisthenics and drills. They endured backbreaking hikes in ninety-five-degree temperatures and ate miserable food. The soldiers also participated in combat drills, crawling through a muddy obstacle course while machine guns fired overhead. For those accustomed to the comforts of civilian life, the military routine was quite a shock. Irving Berlin's song "This Is the Army Mr. Jones" captured the experience of the average soldier:

> This is the army Mr. Jones
> No private rooms or telephones
> You had your breakfast in bed before
> But you won't have it there anymore.

Soldiers in the army came from diverse economic backgrounds and from every ethnic and religious group. Mark Harris and his coauthors wrote in *The Homefront:*

> The collective living experience threw college graduates together with illiterates, Christians with Jews, Catholics with Protestants, Yankees with Southerners, and farm youth with streetwise young men from cities.... Provincialism and regionalism were broken down by the uprooting and mixing of millions of Americans who otherwise might never have traveled beyond their native region.

Many veterans described their time in the army as a vivid learning experience.

There were millions of American men, however, who never served in the military. Many able-bodied men were exempt from service because they worked in vital industries or on farms. Others were exempt because of physical or mental disabilities. Fathers were initially excused from service, but as manpower shortages grew, even they were called up after 1943. There were also thousands of conscientious objectors (COs), men who refused to fight because of their religious or moral beliefs. COs often did public service work instead as medics or medical orderlies, social workers, and smoke jumpers (parachutists who put out forest fires).

These men at home who did not serve in the army still contributed to the war effort, but many were plagued by doubts that they did not measure up to the soldiers at the front. "You didn't want to be out of it," recalled one man. "You didn't want to walk down the street and have people think, he's a slacker. Unless you were in the service or doing a very valuable defense job, you felt a little bit ashamed to tell people what you were doing."

Both men and women on the home front also shouldered another burden. Virtually every American had a family member, friend, or neighborhood acquaintance who had gone off to the front lines. Although people were proud to have a son, husband, or brother in the service, they also experienced tremendous anxiety whenever a loved one went off to combat. American families lived with constant fear and doubt, wondering whether their loved ones were safe. It was perhaps toughest on the young wives whose husbands were in the army. A woman might go as long as two years without seeing her husband, and weeks or

"I Double Dare You"

Listening to the radio was part of the wartime experience for every World War II soldier. Radios were carried aboard ships, to the front lines, and to the base camps. Radio broadcasts helped boost morale and were the foot soldier's only link to the world outside his unit.

The British Broadcasting Company (BBC), located in London, featured interviews with celebrities, comedy programs, and favorite wartime songs. Every night, the BBC broadcast an hour of personal dedications, poems, and phrases that seemed to make little sense to most listeners. In reality, they were coded messages to the French Resistance and to American secret agents. The BBC also reported accurate accounts of the ongoing battles. These were avidly followed by people in the occupied territories whose primary knowledge of the war was from German propaganda reports that exaggerated German victories.

Germany had its own radio station in Paris. It regularly boasted about the German army and taunted the Allies to open a second front. One female broadcaster, called Axis Sally, was widely known for her sexy voice and her outrageous statements. On the eve of the Normandy invasion, she repeatedly broadcast a popular American tune, "I Double Dare You," with new lyrics in English written by the Germans.

I double dare you to come over here
I double dare you to venture too near
Take off your high hat and quit that bragging
Cut out that claptrap and keep your hat on
Can't you take a dare on?

I double dare you to venture a raid
I double dare you to try and invade
And if your loud propaganda
means half of what it says
I double dare you to come over here
I double dare you.

With the help of advertising agencies and the mass media, the U.S. government launched publicity campaigns to build enthusiasm for the war.

even months might go by without a letter. Her children would grow older without ever meeting their father.

War Touched All Americans

Before the war was over, every American knew someone who died or was wounded in combat. The newspapers printed daily lists of soldiers killed in action. And, the obituary columns became the first thing people read in their morning newspapers. Small towns put up monuments and plaques with the names of the local men who had died. A common, disturbing experience for many Americans was to receive a telegram stating that their husband or son had been killed and then to continue receiving delayed letters from that soldier over the next few weeks that assured his family he was fine.

Despite their wartime experiences, Americans almost unanimously supported the war as a fight between good and evil. President Roosevelt claimed:

> We are fighting to cleanse the world of ancient evils, ancient ills. That is the conflict that day and night pervades our lives. No compromise can end the conflict. There has never been—and there can never be—a successful compromise between good and evil. Only total victory can reward the champions of tolerance and decency and freedom and faith.

It was for these reasons that so many Americans came to see World War II as the last of the "good wars." It was the only war in the twentieth century to be overwhelmingly supported by the American people.

The task for FDR and his administration was to transform this moral support into enthusiastic participation in the war effort by every American. The United States was the only participant in World War II that was never bombed or invaded. Its cities were left untouched by the horrible devastation inflicted on Europe, where the the war produced a sense of shared sacrifice and suffering and gave the European population a common purpose. Americans faced no similar danger together, and their personal sacrifices were minimal. But in order to fight a successful war, the government had to find a way to make the American people feel a common resolve.

Federal agencies, with the help of the mass media and advertising agencies, launched a series of well-publicized programs to build enthusiasm for the war. The government persuaded Americans to buy war bonds in denominations ranging from $25 to $10,000. War bonds helped finance the huge costs of the war and allowed Americans to put their extra money into interest-earning savings. Radio advertisements told listeners to "back the attack" by buying the bonds. Movie stars auctioned their personal belongings to raise money. Betty Grable sold her stockings, and Hedy Lamarr offered to kiss anyone who bought $25,000 worth of bonds. War bond rallies with appearances by Charlie Chaplin, Gary Cooper, Bette Davis, and others were held in cities across the nation. The government even used comic strips to convince Americans to buy bonds. Superman, for instance, urged readers to purchase the bonds. War bonds worth nearly $135 billion were purchased during the war. The campaign also helped build national morale and got people directly involved in the war effort.

Citizens Help the War Effort

Other programs generated a more personal feeling of contributing to the war effort. "Victory gardens," for example, sprang up throughout the country. Americans were encouraged to plant vegetable gardens in backyards, in parking lots, and in playgrounds so that mass-produced food could be shipped to the American and Allied troops. With so much food going overseas, the victory gardens were the only way for Americans to enjoy fresh vegetables. By 1943, almost one-third of all vegetables consumed in the United States came from the twenty million victory gardens.

Scrap drives were held to make up for shortages of critical materials. The scraps people donated were recycled into various

Posters like these urged citizens to devote themselves to the war effort and reminded them of the reasons the war was fought.

Government posters urged citizens to buy war bonds to help pay for the costs of the war (above, and below right). High school students in Long Beach, California, lined up on a school playing field to remind citizens to buy bonds during a bond drive (below, left).

weapons. It was said that the iron in a single shovel could be used to make four hand grenades. The most enthusiastic participants in the scrap drives were children. American kids collected tinfoil and aluminum into huge balls that brought fifty cents apiece. One baseball team, the Brooklyn Dodgers, gave free tickets to their games to anyone who brought a piece of scrap iron or metal. Many enterprising youngsters removed an "extra" heating iron or pot from their home to help the war effort—and to enter the ballpark for free.

Millions of Americans also joined the war effort through community civil defense programs. When the war began, German and Japanese submarines patrolled the waters off both American coasts. Many citizens worried about attacks or air raids. There were constant rumors of German and Japanese spies secretly slipping onto American shores. Although the threat of invasion grew remote as the war progressed, in the early years, it was taken seriously by all state and city authorities. Each city and town held mock air raids to prepare its citizens for a possible real attack. A police siren, fire alarm, factory whistle, or train horn would sound to warn the people of the phony raid. Air raid wardens helped gather people into shelters and inspected stores to ensure they had properly prepared buckets of sand to extinguish fires. Volunteer fire fighters and police officers manned their posts. These civil defense volunteers took their jobs seriously and felt proud to be doing their part to win the war. More than twelve million Americans served in some form of civil defense during the war.

Cities on the coasts imposed nighttime curfews and blackouts. The bright lights of the city were visible for miles at sea,

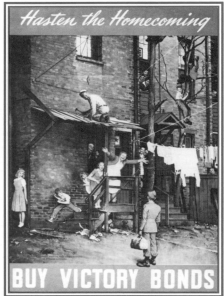

and American ships were silhouetted against this lighted backdrop, making it easy for enemy submarines to spot and sink them. In New York City, all outdoor advertising and neon lights were banned, citizens were forced to shut off their lights after 9:00 P.M., and even the flashy signs of Times Square were dimmed. People used heavy drapes or opaque curtains to shield the windows of their homes. At first, the blackouts were a refreshing experience. People were amazed to be able to see stars in the sky. It became a popular pastime to climb the tallest building or the highest hill to watch the lights go out in the city. Charles Huntington, then a student in Seattle, remembered: "I was standing with a group on a hill overlooking town and it was kind of spooky to watch the city slowly darken until it disappeared. There was no festive mood in our group, just a hushed feeling, as though we were witnessing something that might change our lives. We didn't really understand it, but we felt very vulnerable."

After awhile, however, the blackouts, curfews, and air raid drills became annoying to many Americans. People grew tired of air raid wardens nagging them to "get the lights out" and did not

Americans of all ages, but especially children, collected scrap iron and metal to be used for producing weapons and other necessities of war. Posters of the time (top right) reflected this effort. Even Hollywood celebrities like Rita Hayworth (top left) also joined the scrap effort. Rationing of food and other goods meant long lines, confusing procedures, and a thriving black market.

Benjamin O. Davis

One of the most inspiring stories of the war was the saga of Benjamin O. Davis, Jr., and the Tuskegee Airmen.

In 1941, as an Air Force colonel, Davis assumed command of an all-black fighter group and the Ninety-ninth Pursuit Squadron. The unit was initially assigned only patrol duties because prejudiced white officers believed blacks did not have the proper reflexes to make first-class fighter pilots. Davis was eager to prove his men were capable of flying combat missions.

In the skies over Anzio, the black fighter pilots proved their critics were wrong. They were pressed into combat duties because of a shortage of pilots. On two days in January 1944, the Tuskegee Airmen shot down twelve German fighters. A later study revealed the Ninety-ninth Squadron's combat record equaled that of any other squadron in the Mediterranean campaign. Black pilots flew dangerous missions over Europe for the rest of the war. Benjamin Davis went on to become a three-star general in the Air Force. The Tuskegee Airmen broadened the role that blacks were allowed in the U.S. armed forces. They also helped advance the eventual racial integration that took place in civilian American society.

like having their daily routines disrupted. Many of those who were involved in civil defense activities had never held positions of authority before and were not effective leaders.

Controversial Rationing Program

Americans also did without many food items and other products as a result of mandatory rationing programs. More than thirty essential items—including meat, sugar, nylon stockings, cigarettes, and gasoline—were rationed or regulated during the war. Every American received two ration books for his or her family. One contained blue coupons for canned goods; the other had red coupons for meat, fish, and dairy products. Goods were assigned point values, which went up or down depending on the supply. Every citizen's ration books contained a monthly quota of points that could be allocated as the person pleased. Because of a fuel and rubber shortage, gasoline was also strictly rationed with separate coupon booklets. Pleasure driving was prohibited, and a speed limit of thirty-five miles per hour was imposed.

The rationing program was quite controversial. During World War II, Americans had more money than ever before, but they had nowhere to spend it. The rationing was administered by the federal Office of Price Administration and was always bogged down in confusing procedures. People endured the program with lots of grumbling, and persistent complainers were often greeted with the familiar retort: "Don't you know there's a war on!" Americans learned to live with the system and often resorted to bartering with friends and neighbors, perhaps exchanging unwanted coffee for extra sugar. Of course, there was always the inevitable busybody who threatened to turn the offenders into the ration boards, police, and even the FBI.

Americans also turned to the black market—conducting illegal trades or ignoring official regulations—for those hard-to-find items. As Richard Lingeman, however, has pointed out in *Don't You Know There's a War On:* "The black market was not a clandestine [secret] place, through whose doors slunk furtive citizens. Nor was it a little man whispering 'Psst' through a doorway and then opening his coat to reveal a wealth of precious items.... A good deal of black marketers were legitimate businessmen who evaded price and ration regulations." For a little extra, a merchant could be persuaded to give a customer a better cut of meat, or some extra sugar or cigarettes, or even to find a pair of nylon stockings in a back room somewhere. Organized crime also operated on the black market, often printing and then selling counterfeit ration coupons. Most Americans at one time or another used the black market and tended to ignore the criminal aspects of the practice.

Americans of Japanese descent were viewed as a military threat. Here, a California family awaits transport to a prison camp. Identification tags show on their jackets.

Racial Discrimination

Although solidarity among Americans had never been greater, racial discrimination persisted throughout the war. One-hundred-thousand Japanese-American citizens were placed in prison camps during the war. The government justified the imprisonment by saying that since the country was at war with Japan, these citizens were a military threat. They might act as spies or conduct sabotage. But long-standing racial prejudice was also the reason the Japanese were imprisoned. African-Americans also faced prejudice in the army, workplace, and community. Blacks enlisted and were drafted into the armed forces but were segregated from whites. Black soldiers trained in separate camps, ate in separate mess halls, and formed separate units. Racism ran so deep that the army even segregated the blood plasma of blacks and whites, even though there was no difference in the blood and even though the person who discovered the procedure, Dr. Charles R. Drew, was himself black. Black soldiers also had to endure the indignity and humiliation of discrimination outside the confines of army bases. One black veteran vividly recalled an occasion when he was refused service by a restaurant in Kansas. The soldier was furious when he looked inside and saw that German prisoners of war were allowed to eat there.

Black soldiers were initially restricted to noncombat jobs as laborers, cooks, dishwashers, clerks, and servants. The Air Force and Marine Corps early on prohibited blacks from serving in

Black soldiers were initially restricted to noncombat jobs, but later distinguished themselves in fighting. Here, black Seabees drill in general military maneuvers near Norfolk, Virginia, in 1942.

their ranks at all. White officers persisted in their racist beliefs that blacks could not be trusted in combat and were incapable of leading men into battle. Yet as the war dragged on and casualties mounted, black soldiers were sent up to the front in segregated units. There, black soldiers distinguished themselves and fought honorably in every branch of the armed forces.

In the South, where much of the wartime industry was located, blacks were prohibited from working in the factories. Racial segregation of the schools, public transportation, and restaurants went unchanged. In the North, blacks eventually received jobs in defense factories, but they were discriminated against in terms of wages and promotions. Blacks were also confined to living in segregated slums where rents were high but the housing was run-down. Physical attacks and riots against blacks occurred in many Northern cities. In June 1943, a race riot broke out in Detroit, killing twenty-five blacks and nine whites and injuring eight hundred.

African-Americans deeply resented the continued discrimination and their exclusion from the war effort. They believed it was not right for the United States to fight for democracy abroad when it failed to guarantee equal opportunity and treatment for minorities at home. Civil rights organizations and leaders pressured the Roosevelt administration to enact a fair employment practices bill. FDR issued an executive order banning discrimination based on "race, creed, color or national origin" in defense industries and in government offices. Although the impact of this decree was limited, the idea that government action could be

The Ninety-third Infantry Division, the first all-black division to be formed during World War II, awaits a command to attack during drills.

used to end racial discrimination would be powerfully asserted by civil rights activists such as Martin Luther King, Jr., in the 1950s and 1960s.

Despite the war, Americans still found plenty of ways to amuse themselves. Going to the movies continued to be one of the chief pleasures of the period. Wartime songs on the radio brought the joy and heartache of the war to millions. "We'll Meet Again," "White Cliffs of Dover," and "Lili Marleen," a German song that became popular on both sides, were among the favorites. These ballads told of a rosy future, a world of peace after the fighting stopped. Other popular songs were slightly more realistic. One wartime classic told the true story of a navy chaplain at Pearl Harbor who, when the bombs started falling, took over the antiaircraft gun of a fallen soldier and said, "Praise the Lord and pass the ammunition."

CHAPTER SIX

D Day

In early June 1944, the largest armada the world has ever known lay off the coast of England. The long-awaited invasion of Nazi-occupied France was about to begin. The Allies had assembled five thousand vessels and nearly 1.5 million troops for the attack. Thirteen miles across the English Channel, the embattled Germans gathered behind their own defensive barriers. The struggle for Normandy would be the most important battle on the western front of Europe of the entire war. It would be the last chance for Hitler to salvage his crumbling empire.

Germany had known that an Allied invasion of northern France was inevitable ever since the United States entered the war. During 1943 and 1944, the Germans constructed the "Atlantic wall" to repel the attack. The Germans placed mines on the beaches and in the coastal waters. Jagged wooden logs and metal stakes, all topped with mines, were all along the shores. Mortars and machine guns were in position on the bluffs overlooking the beaches. "Never in the history of modern warfare," wrote historian Cornelius Ryan, "had a more powerful or deadly array of defenses been prepared for an invading force."

Erwin Rommel was named to command the German defenses on the western front. He believed that the first twenty-four hours of the invasion would be critical because the campaigns in North Africa, Sicily, and Italy had proven that once the Allies gained a foothold, they were impossible to dislodge. If the Germans could drive the Allies back into the sea, however, it might be years before they could mount a new assault. And then, Hitler could shift the bulk of his forces to the east to finish the fight with the Soviets.

Although they knew an attack was coming, the Germans had a major disadvantage. They could not predict where or when it would take place. The Allies had decided upon a landing in Normandy, but they mounted a gigantic decoy plan to fool the Germans into believing that the invasion would come at Calais. They leaked information that General Patton, the American general whom the Germans most feared, had been named to command a new army. They constructed a phony army of wooden tanks, planes, and ships in southern England directly across from Calais. They created fake radio messages between nonexistent army units. While the German chief of staff maintained that the attack would come in Normandy, Hitler became convinced that the main invasion would fall in Calais. He refused to send his most experienced troops to the Normandy region. Instead, the German ground forces in Normandy were chiefly staffed by elderly or sick soldiers from the eastern front.

Watching the Weather

The problem that remained for the Allies was deciding when to launch the invasion. The weather was of key importance. Sea landings required low tides, and the airborne operations needed a cloudless, moonlit night. The Allied meteorologic staff calculated that June 5 and 6 met these ideal conditions. All preparations were targeted for those dates. Unfortunately, bad weather on June 4 forced a postponement. This delay greatly increased the physical and mental strain on the soldiers. The men had been cooped up on ships for weeks awaiting the invasion. They were tired of the overcrowded and unsanitary conditions, and many were constantly seasick.

Everyone worried about the fighting to come. It was widely expected that casualties during the landings would be heavy.

French troops train on a North African beach in preparation for the Allied invasion of France (left) and General Eisenhower instructs paratroopers moments before they fly from Great Britain to the European continent for the Allied assault (right).

Each man wondered what his own chances of survival would be. All the soldiers wrote long letters home to their wives, sweethearts, and families. Capt. John Dulgan of Missouri, a veteran of several campaigns, wrote to his wife and children:

> Before the invasion of North Africa, I was nervous and a little scared. During the Sicilian invasion, I was so busy that the fear passed while I was working.... This time we will hit a beach in France and from there God only knows the answer.... I want you to know that I love you with all my heart.... I pray that God will see fit to spare me to you and Ann and Pat.

In the early evening on June 5, General Eisenhower convened a meeting of his top commanders to discuss whether the invasion should go forward the next day as planned. If the bad weather persisted, Eisenhower would be faced with a momentous decision: to chance a landing right away or to put off the assault for at least two weeks until weather conditions would again be favorable. Postponement also entailed risks. The men's morale would deteriorate if they spent more time in their confined quarters. There was also the danger that the secret of the invasion might be leaked in the meantime.

A Gleam of Hope

The Allies' chief meteorologist told Eisenhower and his generals that there was a slight gleam of hope. He believed conditions would improve over France from late at night on June 5 through the afternoon of June 6. It might be possible to make the landings during this period. Eisenhower went around the room and asked each general his opinion: Should the Allies risk the invasion tomorrow or postpone? Of course, the choice was ultimately Eisenhower's. There was a long silence as he sat quietly and considered his options. Finally, he looked up and said, "Well, we'll go." The invasion was on for June 6, 1944.

News of the decision quickly circulated among the Allied troops. Many were relieved that the agonizing waiting was finally over. Even a bloody battle, the soldiers said, could not be any worse than sitting on the ships for another month. Gen. Omar Bradley, who commanded the American troops, shook hands with his infantrymen and gave them his blessing. "I wouldn't miss this show for anything in the world," said Bradley. "Some of you will be killed, but a person who lives through this invasion will be proud for the rest of his life for having been part of it."

Shortly after midnight, French Resistance fighters heard the BBC code announcing the invasion was on. They immediately leaped into action, cutting telephone and telegraph wires throughout Normandy. Many German units were unable to contact or receive information from army headquarters for hours at the start of the invasion. At 2:00 A.M., the Allied airborne divisions set out for France. Their mission was incredibly dangerous. They had to parachute miles into enemy territory and then seize the main bridges and roads leading to the beaches. The paratroopers had to prevent German tanks and reinforcements from reaching the landing sites. Outnumbered by more than three to one, the soldiers hoped the element of surprise would be in their favor. However, if necessary, they would dig in and fight until the infantrymen arrived.

In the noisy planes, the soldiers looked down and saw the reflection of the moonlight shining off the water as they crossed the channel. Once the planes reached the coastline, the German antiaircraft batteries opened fire. The paratroopers saw streams of flashing lights rushing up from the ground, exploding all around them. When the green light in the cabin flashed on, the men hooked their lines to the overhead cable, moved to the door, and hurled themselves into the darkness. All around Normandy, the sky was filled with the wondrous sight of thousands of figures floating to the ground.

The Pathfinders Land

The first to land were the pathfinders. These men quickly set up flashing lights and beacons to mark the drop zones for the other parachutists. Soldiers from the American 82nd and 101st Airborne Divisions dropped into empty fields, gardens, and roadsides. Some men were trapped in trees. Others crashed through greenhouses or were stuck on top of churches. Many of these unfortunate men were killed by the Germans before they could wrestle free of their parachutes.

The Germans were confused by the airborne assault. No one could tell for sure how many men had landed or whether this was the prelude to the big invasion. Communications were difficult because of the work of the French Resistance. The Germans were also fooled because the Americans dropped hundreds of lifelike, rubber dummies dressed as paratroopers south of the Normandy area. Each dummy had a string of firecrackers attached that exploded upon landing. It sounded to the Germans as if a gigantic firefight were raging on their flanks. The troops who rushed to investigate were surprised to find only make-believe opponents.

The American paratroopers faced huge problems right from the start. Due to inexperienced pilots, their forces were widely scattered throughout the Normandy countryside. Some landed as far as twenty miles from their planned destination. Hundreds of Americans were dropped into the artificial swamps that the Germans had created to slow down the Allied offensive. Some soldiers, loaded down with equipment and supplies, drowned in only three feet of water. Half of the heavy artillery and ammunition of the American forces disappeared in these swamps.

Crickets in the Darkness

The American troops were forced to quickly reassemble into fighting units. German patrols were everywhere. In the pitch-black darkness, it was often difficult to distinguish between friend and foe. All Americans carried tiny metal crickets as a recognition signal. If there was no reply to their cricket call, the soldiers had to make a split-second decision to open fire. The men's lives often depended on their quick thinking and reflexes. Fighting was fierce during the night, and the American forces endured high casualties. But they did capture the town of Saint Mere Eglise and secured the roads leading from the beach. Now, it was up to the infantrymen.

The convoy of Allied ships heading toward France stretched as far as the eye could see. Word passed through the ranks of the troops on board that Rome had been liberated by American forces two days earlier, but any celebration was dampened by thoughts of what lay ahead. Soldiers gave the chaplains letters and mementos to pass on to their families in case they were killed. The men wished each other good luck and shook hands, many for the last time. Technical sergeant Roy Stevens of the Twenty-ninth Division searched frantically aboard his crowded ship for his twin brother. Stevens said, "I finally found him. He

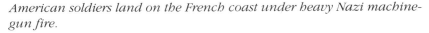

American soldiers land on the French coast under heavy Nazi machine-gun fire.

Members of an American landing party help others whose landing craft was sunk by enemy gunfire. These survivors reached Utah Beach near Cherbourg, France, by using a life raft.

smiled and extended his hand. I said 'No, we will shake hands at the crossroads in France like we planned.' We said good-bye and I never saw him again."

Seven miles off the coast, the infantrymen scrambled over the railings of the transport ships and used the rope webs that stretched alongside to climb to their landing craft. Each assault boat carried thirty-two men. The soldiers were weighted down by more than sixty pounds of gear: rifles, rations, grenades, ammunition, packs of TNT, wire cutters, and shovels. The vessels were rocked by the stormy sea. Waves splashed over the rim of the boats, soaking every soldier to the bone. The men quickly filled up every available bucket, and even their own helmets, with vomit from seasickness.

Three thousand soldiers led the attack. In the first hours, everything depended on how many of these men could cross the beaches and fight their way inland. The hundreds of thousands of soldiers waiting at sea would be unable to land unless these men could make a dent in the German lines. It was truly a dramatic moment. World War II had brought millions of men into conflict using weapons of incredible sophistication. But in the next few hours, the entire fate of the war rested in the hands

New Devices of War

The Normandy invasion featured a wide assortment of military inventions specially designed for the attack. Small landing craft were built to ferry the soldiers to the beaches. Amphibious tanks could swim to shore, and tanks with large steel projectiles were used to clear away heavy obstacles. Soldiers used long metal tubes containing explosives, known as bangalore torpedoes, to clear away barbed wire.

Perhaps the most impressive of all were the two structures that were towed across the English Channel to the Normandy beaches. These structures, known as Mulberries, were gigantic artificial harbors. The harbors allowed the Allied ships to unload troops and supplies off-shore. Before the harbors were invented, ships had to hazard a beach landing. They were an engineering miracle and one of the biggest secrets of the invasion. Forty-five thousand men labored day and night to complete the work in time. The harbors stretched almost two miles wide and assured the constant flow of men and supplies into the beachhead after the initial landings.

Pointe du Hoc

On D day, one of the most important Allied objectives was to capture a one-hundred-foot cliff located midway between the Utah and Omaha beaches. Allied intelligence believed the Germans had placed there a battery of six huge guns that could devastate the landings on both beaches. An elite squad of two hundred army Rangers was to land on the small beach at the foot of the bluffs, climb to the summit, and capture the guns.

The Rangers encountered heavy fire upon landing, and one landing craft capsized. The men scrambled to the beach and used specially fitted mortars to fire rope ladders with hooks to the top of the cliffs. They then rushed forward and began climbing up the steep face of the bluff. German soldiers suddenly appeared on top and began to spray machine-gun fire and throw hand grenades down upon the helpless Americans. The Germans cut the ropes, and many Rangers fell to their death.

Still, some of the soldiers made their way up the rocks. Five minutes after their landing, enough Rangers reached the summit to secure the ropes and disperse the German forces. However, to their dismay, they discovered the enemy stronghold was empty. The Germans had moved the weapons inland several days earlier.

The assault on Omaha Beach left many dead and wounded Americans. Here, injured members of the Sixteenth Infantry Regiment await evacuation after the assault.

of these few, brave men. Like all battles, the success of D day—the day of the Normandy invasion—would depend on simple acts of bravery and courage by individual soldiers.

A Lucky Occurrence

At about 6:30 A.M., the first troops reached shore. The American landings at Utah Beach went remarkably well, with little opposition from the Germans. Trained engineers cleared the beach of obstacles and mines. Almost all of the heavy artillery and amphibious tanks reached shore safely. By midnight, the troops had captured an area of four square miles. Of the 23,000 men who landed that day at Utah Beach, there were only 197 casualties. As luck would have it, the Americans landed in the wrong place, almost a mile from the original destination. They were fortunate because the Germans had concentrated their heavy artillery and troops at the original site. Although the British and Canadians encountered stiffer resistance sixteen miles away at Gold, Juno, and Sword beaches, they too were able to move inland at a fast pace.

Ten miles away, the Americans on Omaha Beach faced an entirely different battlefield. The landing there was an absolute nightmare. Allied bombardment in the early hours of the invasion failed to destroy the German artillery batteries. The Germans had also moved an experienced regiment into position overlooking the beaches. When the soldiers reached within two hundred yards of the shore, the German guns opened fire. Numerous landing craft took direct hits and exploded into flames. Others were destroyed when they ran into mines or capsized after ramming underwater obstacles. When the first wave of soldiers hit the beaches, the Germans fired artillery shells and mortars from the hills. Fire from hidden machine-gun nests blasted every inch of the beach. In the first few minutes, nearly one-third of the soldiers were hit before reaching the beach. Entire companies were killed in a matter of moments.

Hundreds of Bloated Bodies

The soldiers were pinned down at the water's edge by a wall of murderous fire. Men took cover behind the beach obstacles and the bodies of their dead comrades. One soldier remembered the horrible scene: "It seemed we had entered hell itself. The whole beach was a great burning fury. All around were burning vehicles, puffed up bodies, the swimming tanks. None of them had made it to shore. Flames were coming from them. The water was burning."

The second and third incoming waves of soldiers were subjected to the same horror. The water was covered with hundreds of floating helmets and bloated bodies. Wrecked landing craft began to pile up offshore in a watery graveyard. By 7:00 A.M., the American attack was a complete shambles. None of the men had

Crossed rifles in the sand are a comrade's tribute to an American soldier who died in the Allied assault.

D Day

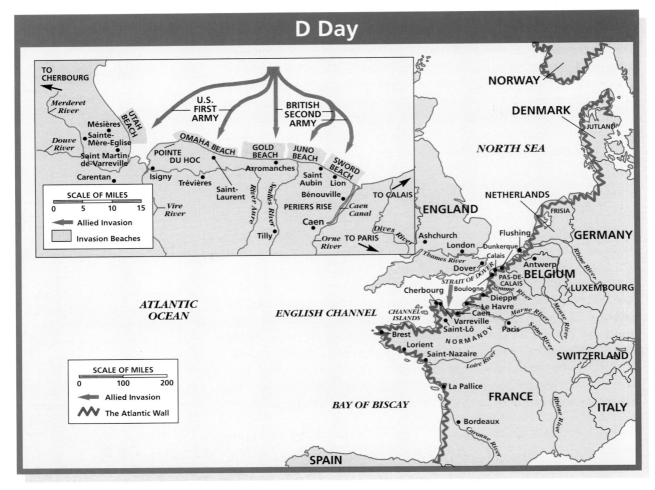

advanced off the beach, and no attacks had been launched against the German fortifications.

An hour later, things were at a standstill. The soldiers had crawled up to a three-foot-high seawall that offered some protection from the German guns. Anyone who dared raise his head was picked off by German sharpshooters. The boats carrying the demolition engineers were destroyed, so mines still littered the shore. Almost all of the amphibious tanks launched offshore had sunk into the water.

The Omaha landings, like the landings at the other beaches, had been organized according to a precise schedule. The fifty thousand troops waiting offshore were unable to land unless some progress was made. General Bradley, who was on the bridge of the cruiser *Augusta* a few thousand yards off Omaha Beach, received his first account of the battle at 10:00 A.M. The reports were entirely negative, and Bradley considered diverting the next landing force to Utah Beach. This would mean abandoning the American forces already on Omaha Beach and admitting that this landing was a failure.

The Shock of Battle

By this time, the troops from the initial waves had been pinned down behind the seawall for two or three hours. The dead and wounded lay everywhere, and mortar rounds and artillery shells continued to land on the beach. The men were too stunned by the speed of events to move forward. They were completely paralyzed with shock and fear. One sergeant said he "came upon a man sitting at the edge of the water, seemingly unaware of the machine gun fire which ripped all over the area. He sat there throwing stones into the water and softly crying as if his heart would break." In every battle, every person's instinct, especially for inexperienced soldiers, is to take cover under fire. For the soldiers at Omaha Beach, this instinct was reinforced by the sight of the bodies of all the soldiers who had failed to do so. In such a situation, it takes considerable courage to keep moving.

But the Americans realized they had to get off the beach or they would die. Brig. Gen. Norman Cota, a fifty-one-year-old veteran, ran up and down the length of the seawall urging the men to renew their attack. Soldiers who were crouched behind the wall were amazed that the brash general was not killed. Some

A huge Nazi gun battery, with concrete walls thirteen feet thick, was silenced by the bombs of Allied flyers carrying out their missions over France.

A Close-up View

In World War II photographs could be instantly transmitted across oceans by radar and across continents by telegraph wire. Photographs of battles often appeared in American and British newspapers the day after the fighting took place. Magazines such as *Life, Look, Collier's,* and *Harper's Weekly* brought the hardships and triumphs of the distant war directly into American living rooms with their photos.

Photojournalists traveled with the Allied troops wherever they went. Their profession was often incredibly dangerous.

Life photographer Robert Capa was one of the journalists who accompanied the first wave of invaders that landed in Normandy. Like the soldiers, he took refuge from the intense German fire by hiding behind a wrecked tank. He wrote:

After 20 minutes, I suddenly realized that the tanks were a certain amount of cover from the small arms fire but that they were what the Germans were shooting shells at, so I made for the beach. I fell down.... It was very unpleasant there and having nothing else to do, I started shooting pictures.

The photos Capa took on Omaha Beach that day became some of the most celebrated images of the war.

A soldier's gun and helmet, standing on the battered Normandy beach, form a poignant tribute to a dead American soldier.

took heart by his example and began moving. Other courageous soldiers dodged bullets and crawled forward to clear paths through the barbed-wire obstacles. Small groups pushed inland and encircled the German machine-gun posts. An American destroyer, the *Frankford,* moved close to shore and directed its guns against the Germans. After the intense bombardment, many of the Germans fled their strongholds and surrendered. Slowly, the tide of the battle turned. By late afternoon, Omaha Beach was secured, and more troops began to land.

The day after the battle, Ernie Pyle wandered along Omaha Beach. He wrote:

The strong, swirling tides of the Normandy coastline shift the contours of the sandy beach as they move in and out. They carry soldiers' bodies out to sea and later they return them. They cover the corpses of heroes with sand, and then in their whims they uncover them. As I plowed out over the wet sand of the beach on that first day ashore, I walked around what seemed to be a couple of pieces of driftwood sticking out of the sand. But they weren't driftwood. They were a soldier's two feet. He was completely covered by the shifting sands except for his feet. The toes of his G.I. shoes pointed toward the land he had come so far to see, and which he saw so briefly.

The dead lay on the beach where they fell. There was not enough time to bury them. Wreckage was littered along miles of shoreline. Diaries, Bibles, letters from home, snapshots of loved ones, and other personal belongings were scattered in the sand. The human cost of June 6 was high. The Americans suffered 4,649 casualties this first day in Normandy; the Allies altogether had close to 10,000 casualties. But these deaths were not in vain. Within a month, one million men would be able to land in France. Within the year, Allied troops would capture Berlin and Hitler would be dead.

CHAPTER SEVEN

The Allied Drive to the Rhine

In the first days following D day, the Allied beachhead in Normandy was, in many places, less than one mile deep. The Allies' most pressing task was to unite all the separate forces as quickly as possible. The American forces linked up on June 10, and two days later, the Allied armies were in continuous contact along a fifty-mile front. The Allies' grand strategy called for a fast breakout from Normandy, followed by a massive frontal assault to the Rhine River, the western frontier of Germany, by autumn.

The Allies' greatest concern was whether their forces on the Normandy beachhead would be strong enough to withstand a ferocious counterattack from the Germans. Yet during the first critical weeks of the battle for Normandy, the Germans did not throw the full weight of their army against the Allied forces. Hitler still believed the Allied landings in Normandy were simply a decoy and that the main invasion would fall in Calais. He refused to commit his vital panzer reinforcements north of the Seine River to Normandy. It was not until late June that Hitler reluctantly admitted Normandy would be the decisive battlefield. By then, however, it was too late to drive the Allies back into the sea.

By late June, twenty-five Allied divisions were ashore, with another fifteen in England awaiting their departure to France. They were opposed in Normandy at first by only fourteen German divisions. Nevertheless, the Allies found their progress was slow. The Americans did not capture the harbor city of Cherbourg until June 29. The British were delayed in capturing Caen, ten miles from the Normandy beachhead, until July 18, forty-one

(top) An Allied soldier discovers the body of a dead German soldier slumped in a doorway as if asleep. (bottom) American gunners shell retreating German forces near Carentan, France, in July 1944. One soldier protects his ear from the loud blast of the howitzer.

days after D day. The Allied generals had originally forecast that the Allied forces would be 65 miles further, or halfway to the Loire River by this date.

Brutal Combat

The German army fought with their customary skill and persistence. Their tanks were far superior to their Allied counterparts. They also enjoyed a substantial advantage provided by the Normandy countryside. Each farm field was surrounded on all sides by immense, ten-foot-high hedgerows. These were earthen banks with densely intertwined trees, branches, and bushes. Tanks could not penetrate the hedgerows, which offered perfect cover for the German soldiers. The Germans dug trenches behind the hedgerows, where infantrymen with rifles could remain unseen. Snipers hid in the trees, and machine guns were placed at opposite ends of the hedgerow. In this way, the Germans could establish a strong, defensive position every two hundred yards. Once their defenses were in danger of being

(left) An aerial view shows a section of the Siegfried Line, its concrete barriers aligned like sharks' teeth. The German SS troops vowed never to let the Allied forces cross this barrier. (right) A squad of American infantrymen pose with a captured Nazi flag in front of a wrecked German tank.

overrun, they simply retreated to the next field and took cover behind another hedgerow. The countryside became one potential death trap after another for the Allied soldiers.

The Allied advance had to be slow and cautious. There were no dramatic charges across the open fields by an entire platoon, a scene frequently shown in the movies. Instead, small groups of soldiers crept along the hedgerows, a few yards at a time. Although the American soldiers had been trained not to fire their weapons until they spotted the enemy, that tactic was useless in this case. When soldiers reached within firing distance of a hedgerow, they opened fire with grenades, mortars, and rifles. While the German forces were pinned down, other Allied troops crept alongside the hedgerows to knock out the machine guns and get behind the German lines. Sometimes, the remaining German forces surrendered without a fight. Others made a break for another field and were shot down. Some positions had to be fought for until the last man was killed or taken. The entire war in Normandy became a series of more than a thousand small skirmishes scattered across the entire front.

In many ways, the brutal combat in the countryside resembled the horror of the fighting on the eastern front. One soldier remembered: "You are so dulled by fatigue that the names of the killed and the wounded they checked off each night, the names of the men who had been your best friends, might have come out of a phone book for all you know. All the old values were gone and if there was a world beyond this tangle of hedgerows, you never expected to see it." The soldiers in France also had another handicap. They knew they were fighting in a war that was nearly won, but they also knew that this final victory would not be achieved for some time and the chances of getting killed were still great. Volunteers for hazardous duties became less and less frequent. There was a significant increase in battle fatigue and sickness, and many more soldiers were deserting. Even the veterans who had already fought in North Africa and Italy were affected by the strain of combat. "These men had seen actual war at first hand, seeing their buddies killed day after day, trying to tell themselves that they are different—*they* won't get it," wrote Bill Mauldin, "but knowing deep inside that *they* can get it—these guys know what real weariness of body, brain and soul can be."

On July 25, the Allies launched their major offensive to break out of Normandy. The American divisions were split into the First Army, commanded by Gen. Courtney Hodges, and the Third Army, led by Patton. British and Canadian forces under General Montgomery attacked across a broad front near Caen. Patton's forces made spectacular progress to the west, driving the Germans completely out of Brittany. In early August, Patton's army swung back to the north, threatening to trap the entire German army in a pocket near Falaise. Hitler ignored his generals' advice to let the German forces retreat to a defensive position beyond the Seine River. Instead, he ordered the German army to stand and fight in yet another useless effort.

The subsequent battle, known as the Battle of Falaise Gap, was the largest clash of armor in any fight on the western front. Only the gigantic tank battle at Khursk, in the Soviet Union, in 1943 was larger. Across eight hundred miles of countryside, twenty armored divisions, involving almost fifteen hundred tanks, waged battle. Although they put up a valiant fight, the greatly outnumbered German forces were slowly squeezed into a tiny pocket by the Allied troops. The Allies had complete air superiority, and they bombed the German forces around the clock. The high ground to the northwest became known as the "balcony of death," as unopposed artillery crews lobbed shell

(left) Soldiers of the U.S. Seventh Army line up on the massive barrel of a 274-mm railroad gun captured from the Nazis in 1945. (right) A young airman poses for a visual tribute from his unit to the Allies. Names of the Allied nations had been written on bombs destined for Axis targets.

(top left) French military leaders march proudly in the victory parade in Paris after France is freed from Nazi occupation. (top right) Crowds of jubilant Parisians cheer American troops parading along the Champs-Elysees after the liberation of France in 1944. (bottom left) An American tank crew drives through the Arc de Triomphe in Paris after driving the Nazis out of France.

after shell into the German lines below. The French roads and countryside were littered with thousands of corpses, smashed tanks and jeeps, and dead horses and cattle. "It was literally possible to walk for hundreds of yards," said Eisenhower after visiting the battlefield, "stepping on nothing but dead and decaying flesh." The battle ended on August 20. One hundred thousand Germans were killed, and another fifty thousand were taken prisoner. Of the fifty German divisions that were active in June, only ten remained.

The Allies' Liberation of Paris

Ever since D day, thousands of armed fighters in the French Resistance had risen up against the Germans. They sabotaged railroad transportation, ambushed troop convoys, and harassed army garrisons. As the Allies were achieving their smashing victory at Falaise Gap, Communist-led forces of the Resistance seized public buildings in Paris on August 19. Barricades constructed of sandbags, cars, and street stones sprung up throughout the city. Gen. Charles de Gaulle, leader of the Free French Army, viewed the uprising as an attempt by the Communists to seize power. He pressured the Allied command to immediately drive on the French capital. Eisenhower had initially intended to bypass the city, but he gave the order to go ahead. On August 24, French general Jacques Leclerc's Second Armored Division broke through the German defenses and became the first Allied unit to enter Paris. The German commander of Paris, Gen. Dietrich Cholitz, had been ordered by Hitler to raze the beautiful city before retreating, but he disobeyed and agreed to a cease-fire.

On August 25, the American troops marched in triumph down the Champs-Elysees, the main street of Paris. The soldiers were mobbed by the deliriously happy Parisians. People cried out, "We've waited so long for you." Every soldier had at least one woman or young girl on his arm, hugging him, kissing his grimy face, and marching alongside. Parisians shook their hands and slapped their backs. People everywhere were yelling and laughing, throwing flowers and holding up huge bottles of wine for the soldiers to drink. Ernie Pyle recalled: "One funny little old woman—so short she couldn't reach up to kiss men in military vehicles…appeared on the second day carrying a stepladder and let the boys have it with hugs, laughs and kisses." The crowd lifted the soldiers and carried them into cafes and bars. It was an exhilarating outpouring of joy and emotion, a moment that every American soldier would treasure forever.

After the liberation of Paris, the Allied forces continued their march to the Rhine. The Allies fought along a broad front, with the British and Canadian forces to the north and the American First, Third, and Ninth armies spreading southward. Brussels and Antwerp in Belgium were liberated, and all of Belgium and Luxembourg were in Allied hands by mid-September. On the eastern front, the Soviets were defeating the Germans. The Red Army's summer offensive pushed forward 250 miles in three weeks, destroying twenty-eight German divisions. The Soviets then moved in and overturned pro-Nazi regimes in Hungary, Romania, Bulgaria, and Yugoslavia. By the fall, the Red Army reached the banks of the Vistula River, outside of Warsaw, Poland.

With the unparalleled success on both fronts, there was a widespread feeling of elation and expectation among the ranks of American soldiers that the war would be over soon. But the Allied momentum slowed in late September. The rapid advance in the

(top) American infantry secure territory in Belgium on a snowy winter day in January 1945. (bottom left) American soldiers await further orders near the safety of a tank during an advance on a Belgian village in September 1944. (bottom right) Allied soldiers engage the enemy from behind a bunker of parsnips in a field in Holland in 1944.

Hitler's Secret Weapons

Throughout the early years of the war, there were constant rumors that the Nazis were developing secret weapons that would guarantee their victory. In the late 1930s, the Nazis established a scientific research center on the tiny Baltic island of Peenemunde. Their major task was to develop rockets or missiles that could strike faraway targets in England. By 1943, mass production of Germany's V-1 and V-2 rockets was already underway. In June 1943, however, the British air force attacked the island, severely damaging production and setting the program back by months. It was not until June 12, 1944, six days after the Normandy invasion, that the rockets were again ready to fly.

The V-1 was a pilotless flying bomb that was launched from a fixed ramp and guided by automatic pilot. Londoners learned to fear the characteristic buzzing sound of the V-1 that warned of its approach. When a V-1 neared its target, its engine would abruptly shut off. Then, it would fall into a steep dive and explode fifteen seconds later upon reaching the ground. The agonizing wait between the deadly silence and the subsequent explosion terrified the British population. Antiaircraft guns and the RAF were able to knock down thirty-five hundred rockets, but sixty-seven hundred bombs reached London. These killed six thousand people and destroyed twenty-five hundred homes.

The V-2 rockets, on the other hand, fell without any warning. Their original launchpads in northern France were never used because of the Allied invasion. The Germans set up new firing sites in the Netherlands, from where the V-2s could barely reach London. Almost eleven hundred rockets hit the city, killing twenty-seven hundred and wounding another sixty-five hundred. Greater devastation was avoided because the Allied armies made such swift progress and captured most of the Netherlands by September 1944.

A German V-1 guided missile, popularly known as a buzz bomb, is displayed in a town square after the war. London was a favorite target of thousands of these missiles during World War II.

previous six weeks had created a tremendous strain on their supply lines. All supplies were still being brought ashore across the invasion beaches. The Allies improvised a 350-mile supply convoy, nicknamed the Red Ball Express. Trucks raced day and night along a 700-mile circuit. The drivers pushed their vehicles to the limit, competing with each other to see who could finish the journey in the shortest time. Despite their efforts, the American armies ran out of fuel, and the entire Allied offensive came to a halt.

It was six weeks before the supply problems were straightened out. In the meantime, disagreement broke out within the Allied command over strategy. British general Montgomery believed he had a plan that could win the war quickly. He proposed a lightning thrust through the Netherlands into the Ruhr Valley, Germany's industrial heartland. It would eliminate the threat of Germany's terror weapons, the V-1 and V-2 rockets, which were being hurled against England from bases in the Netherlands. The attack would also cripple Germany's war economy, which meant Germany would not be able to continue the war. Montgomery's plan required American reinforcements and an immediate priority in supplies. The American generals thought they deserved their fair share of the supplies and wanted to continue fighting along a broad front. Patton bluntly stated that his Third Army could be in Berlin within a month if his forces received enough fuel.

After heavy lobbying from Churchill, Eisenhower sided with the British general and gave his approval to the daring plan. Montgomery's operation required the seizure of three bridges at vital river crossings, including one over the Rhine at a Dutch town called Arnhem. This so-called "bridge too far" became the most conspicuous Allied failure of the war. If Montgomery's plan had been successful, it might have shortened the war by months, but instead it ended in tragedy. American commandos captured the first two bridges, but the British paratroopers unfortunately landed four miles from the bridge at Arnhem. They fought their way into the town, but unexpectedly found two SS panzer divisions guarding the approaches to the bridge. Against desperate odds, one British unit was able to seize control of the northern end of the bridge for three days. Without the element of surprise, and facing heavy German pressure, the British forces had no choice but to withdraw. Of the ten thousand paratroopers who originally landed, only two thousand escaped. One thousand men were killed, and seven thousand were captured. Any Allied hopes for a quick end to the war disappeared at Arnhem.

Troops ferrying across the Rhine River into Germany in March 1945 huddle for safety as German troops fire on them.

Nearing Germany

Nevertheless, by November 1944, the Allied armies were poised to invade Germany from the west, and the Red Army was approaching from the east. The border town of Aachen became

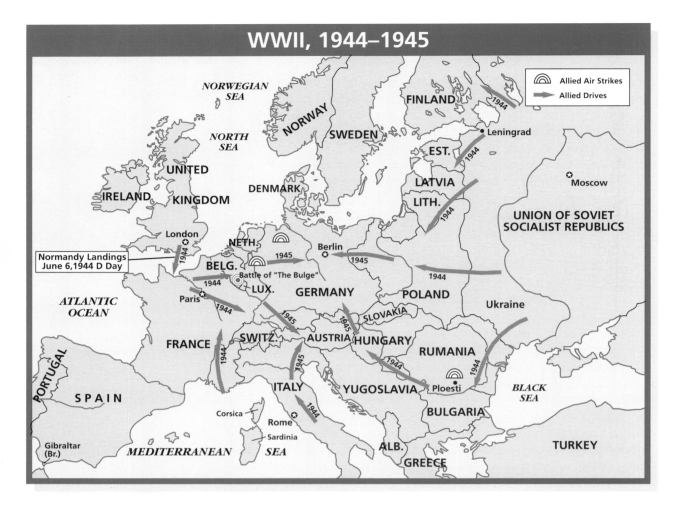

WWII, 1944–1945

Legend:
- Allied Air Strikes
- Allied Drives

Normandy Landings
June 6, 1944 D Day

Battle of "The Bulge"

the first German territory to be captured by American forces on October 29. Yet the closer the Americans came to Germany, the stiffer the Nazi defenses they faced. Hitler called up all remaining able-bodied German men from ages sixteen to sixty-five to serve in the army. Even youngsters from the Hitler Youth were pressed into service. It seemed impossible that these fresh-faced boys, some no older than fourteen, could actually be soldiers, but their units fought with an extraordinary fierceness that rivaled even that of SS units. Diehard SS regiments manned the Siegfried Line, a series of defensive strongholds along the Rhine, and vowed to fight to their last breath.

The Allies continued to make slow progress, but by December, a dangerous gap had opened up between the American First and Third armies. The sector of the Ardennes Forest, which lay between the two armies, was protected by only a single American corps. Two of its three infantry divisions had received heavy casualties in recent fighting and had been sent to the Ardennes to recuperate. A third division was made up of inexperienced soldiers. Allied headquarters, repeating the mistake of the French

An Allied infantryman slips under the barbed wire barricade that stretches between advancing U.S. forces and Nazi positions in Belgium in 1945.

generals in 1940, did not fear an attack through the supposedly impenetrable Ardennes. Likewise, Eisenhower had been assured by his intelligence staff that the Germans would be unable to mount an offensive anytime soon.

Hitler's Desperate Gamble

What the Allies failed to count on was Hitler's fondness for desperate gambles. Pressured on both fronts, he believed his only hope lay in throwing all of his forces and reserves into a reckless offensive against the American army. In mid-November, he informed his generals that the German army would mount an all-out attack through the Ardennes region. The Germans gathered 275,000 men and one thousand tanks, in utmost secrecy, including all their reserves and key units that were relocated from the Soviet front. Hitler's plan was to split the Allied armies in two by capturing Antwerp. The British and Canadian forces would be forced to evacuate to England, and once the Americans were isolated, Hitler believed they would abandon Europe and turn their full attention to the Pacific theater. Germany could then shift all its armies to the eastern front for a final battle with the Red Army. Although impressive on paper, in reality, the plan was completely unrealistic. The German army was ill equipped and woefully outnumbered by the Allies. Similarly, Hitler's belief that the Americans would leave Europe if they suffered severe losses was nothing but a dream.

Still, Hitler had the element of surprise in his favor. On the morning of December 16, the Fifth and Sixth panzer armies fell on the American lines like a hammer. Troops in the north were completely overrun, and they surrendered. Small bands of American soldiers to the south were cut off from their units but waged a good fight that delayed the German onslaught. The American soldiers had come a long way since Kasserine Pass two years earlier. Now, they stood their ground no matter what the odds and fought with professionalism, skill, and courage.

In part, the Americans' will to fight was also a response to news of the killing of ninety American prisoners of war at Malmedy by the Germans on December 17. An SS division, commanded by the twenty-nine-year-old Col. Jochen Peiper, captured a pocket of American troops. His soldiers herded the 150 prisoners into an open field, where machine guns shot them down in cold blood. Soldiers who were only wounded lay completely still on the snowy ground and pretended to be dead. Once the Germans left, the shocked survivors straggled back to the American lines where they told their story to reporters. News of the Malmedy massacre spread like wildfire through the American ranks and helped stiffen the resolve of the American soldiers to defeat the Nazis.

German Spies

In the first days of the battle, reports that German commandos dressed in American uniforms were launching attacks behind American lines also caused great alarm among the troops. At Hitler's personal suggestion, German soldiers who spoke English and were familiar with American slang dressed as GIs and carried out raids behind the American lines. Although there were only a few acts of sabotage, the tactic created tremendous confusion among the Americans. Wild rumors spread that a squadron of German assassins who spoke perfect English was on its way to kill Eisenhower, who remained under heavy guard for a week. Nervous American GIs conducted security checks and interrogated passersby to verify that they were "real Americans." They asked people to name the capital of Montana or say who won the World Series in 1943—questions they assumed no German could possibly know the answers to. But, of course, not even every American could answer all the questions correctly, which created some awkward moments. One "suspected" German was being led off by military police when he began cursing in such strong language that everyone realized that he was a genuine American. German soldiers who were captured in American uniforms were shot as spies.

The German surprise attack drove a thirty-mile bulge in the American front lines. As a result, the fighting in the Ardennes became known as the Battle of the Bulge. The key to the German offensive was the Fifth Panzer Army's attempt to capture the town of Bastogne, a vital road junction. On December 18, a German division reached within two miles of the town, but at night, the 101st Airborne Division raced one hundred miles at breakneck speed to provide reinforcements. Although completely surrounded, the embattled Americans held out for seven days against repeated assaults. On December 22, the German demand to surrender was greeted with Gen. Joseph McAuliffe's legendary rejoinder: "Nuts!" Eisenhower ordered Patton to stop his attack in the south and help break the siege at Bastogne. In seventy-two hours, the entire Third Army swung around in a ninety-degree turn and marched to the town. On the day after Christmas, Patton's men broke through the German lines and saved Bastogne.

It was the turning point of the Battle of the Bulge. During the next few weeks, the Americans counterattacked from both flanks and crushed the German armies. By January 15, 1945, the German forces were utterly destroyed. Their reserves were totally wiped out, and 120,000 were killed or wounded. None of these losses could possibly be made up at this stage of the war. The Battle of the Bulge was a shortsighted gamble by Hitler that merely bought a little time at a great cost. The battle only briefly delayed the Allies from breaking through into Germany and allowed the Red Army to advance in the east virtually unimpeded. It was Hitler's last attempt to save his crumbling empire.

CHAPTER EIGHT

The Fall of the Third Reich

By 1945, the end of the war was near. The German army had been shattered in 1944. One million men had been killed on the western front alone. Still, Hitler rejected any talk of surrender. He envisioned dying in a final blaze of glory. His last days would become a heroic last stand that would be remembered for hundreds of years. Like all dictators, Hitler felt his personal fate was linked with that of his country. "If the war is lost, the German nation must perish," he told Albert Speer, Germany's armaments minister. Hitler ordered Speer to implement a "scorched earth" policy, which called for all German bridges, factories, refineries, mines, power stations, and farms to be set on fire. Nothing would be left for the Allies to capture or destroy. Every German soldier was ordered to stay at his post and fight to the last breath.

In early January, Hitler moved into an underground bunker that had been constructed fifty-five feet beneath a government building. It contained conference rooms, kitchens, living quarters, and electricity and water supplies. Aside from two brief visits aboveground, Hitler did not leave the bunker for 105 consecutive days. He hardly slept, and his health was quickly deteriorating. Hitler gave the impression of being totally insane. He had managed to convince himself that by some miracle the final catastrophe of military defeat could be avoided. Isolated from the sight of Berlin, which was rapidly being destroyed above him, Hitler continually denied the grim reports he received from his generals. Hitler even turned to astrology in the hope that there might be some sign of the great miracle in the stars.

(above) Allied Gen. Bernard Montgomery greets his troops upon entering a German town devastated by the Allied offensive.

(below, top) Thousands of mourners gather in Washington, D.C., for President Franklin D. Roosevelt's funeral on April 14, 1945. Roosevelt died only three weeks before Germany surrendered. (below, bottom) Americans from all walks of life grieve the loss of their president as they line a Washington street to catch a glimpse of his funeral cortege.

Yet there was to be no last-minute victory for Hitler or Nazi Germany. The Allied armies in the west and the Red Army in the east were poised for the final confrontation. The war would be over in a matter of months. The Red Army, after a spectacular advance in the fall, stood a mere thirty-five miles away from Berlin, but the Soviet attack had been stalled at the Oder River for months. The bulk of the remaining German forces had been shifted to the east to prevent a Soviet breakthrough. This opened the door for the Americans in the west, where three million soldiers were preparing to cross the Rhine. The American campaign would be the last great offensive of the war.

On March 7, 1945, an American advance unit captured a railroad bridge over the Rhine at Remagen. German demolition engineers were preparing to detonate explosives on the bridge when American soldiers rushed across and defused the bombs. Over the next several weeks, the American armies poured across the bridge at Remagen and other makeshift pontoon bridges along the Rhine. The First, Third, and Ninth armies made spectacular progress through central Germany. By April 1, the Ruhr Valley was completely encircled. Three weeks later, all resistance ended and 325,000 German soldiers were taken prisoner, the largest capture of the war. Throughout April, the American forces

Holocaust: Nazi Germany's War Against the European Jews

The most tragic event of the war was the murder of millions of innocent European Jews by the Nazis for the sake of racial purity. All in all, six million Jews, fully 40 percent of the world's Jewish population, were exterminated during the war.

Anti-Semitism, or racial prejudice against Jews, had been an important feature of Nazi ideology from the outset. German Jews were blamed for Germany's defeat in World War I. Under Hitler's regime, they were prohibited from holding jobs as teachers, lawyers, civil servants, or doctors. They were beaten on the streets by Nazi storm troopers. Many Jews, along with Gypsies, homosexuals, trade unionists, and political opponents of the Nazis, were sent to prisons known as concentration camps. Members of each group were identified by a different "badge" sewn on their prison uniform. For example, Jews wore a yellow star of David; homosexuals a pink triangle. At the beginning of the war, there were about twenty-five thousand prisoners in the camps.

When the invasion of the Soviet Union began, special squads of SS troops followed behind the advancing German forces. They executed as many Soviet Jews as possible. The SS men machine-gunned their victims in huge trenches, which the prisoners themselves were forced to dig beforehand. Others were locked in sealed vans and then gassed to death with carbon monoxide pumped in from the van's engine. It was not until January 1942, however, that plans for the systematic murder of all the Jews in Europe were finalized. High-ranking Nazis met in Wannsee, a suburb of Berlin. The Nazis were careful to use vague, bureaucratic language in their discussions. The proposed mass murder of the Jews was described as "the final solution of the Jewish question" or "resettlement." Even up to the very last months of the war, Nazi Germany diverted precious resources

(left) Front-page propaganda from a Nuremberg newspaper aims to discredit German Jews. (right) The emaciated condition of these concentration camp survivors is testimony to the inhuman treatment they received at the hands of the Nazis.

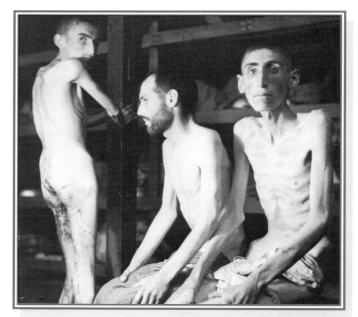

away from military operations to accomplish their despicable mission.

The concentration camps were turned over to a special branch of the SS, the "death's head" divisions, under the direct authority of Heinrich Himmler, the head of the SS. Many of the original concentration camps, such as Dachau, Belsen, and Auschwitz, were transformed into gigantic labor camps. Jews and Soviet prisoners of war were forced to work in abominable conditions until they died. Other camps, such as Belzec, Chelmno, Treblinka, Sobidor, and Majdanek, had no purpose other than to be a site for the murder of Jews. In these death camps, all prisoners were killed as soon as they arrived. Many of these camps were located in rural, eastern Poland, away from prying eyes and where the native population was largely anti-Semitic and unconcerned about the Jews' fate.

Jews from all over Europe were rounded up and transported by cattle cars to the camps. Upon arrival at the death camp, all prisoners were told they had to undergo a "delousing" process after their long train journey. SS guards quickly herded the Jews into specially constructed "showers," with as many as two thousand to a room. The doors were barred, and the SS men poured cyanide gas into the chambers. The corpses were plundered for their gold teeth and fillings, and hair was removed so that it could be used to stuff German pillows and mattresses. The bodies were then thrown into furnaces. The stench of charred human flesh hung over the camps like a dark cloud.

At the labor camps, Jews underwent a selection process that cruelly separated families. Nazi officers took great pleasure in playing God, deciding who would live and who would die. They personally examined every prisoner and then pointed to lines stretching on the left and the right. The elderly, children, pregnant women, and sick men were sent to the left and were immediately gassed. Able-bodied men and women were sent to the right and put to work doing backbreaking labor for sixteen to eighteen hours a day. The sign over the entrance to Auschwitz read: "Arbeit Macht Frei" (Work Makes Freedom). Slave laborers produced armaments, vehicles, and rubber for leading German businesses, such as Mercedes, Siemens, Krupp, and I. G. Farben. Prisoners either died or collapsed from exhaustion, in which case they, too, were sent to the gas chambers.

Some prisoners were selected to be guinea pigs in cruel, inhumane scientific experiments conducted by the Nazi doctors. Those who were fortunate enough to survive—and that was very few—were scarred for life by the experience.

Every person in Europe knew of the extermination of the Jews. Most people in Germany and the occupied countries did not care about the Jews and pretended as if they knew nothing of the camps. Yet there was a handful of courageous people who risked their lives to hide Jews. One of those people in Amsterdam hid the family of Anne Frank, the girl whose diary records her courageous efforts to survive. The entire population of a small village in France, Le Chambon, safely hid five thousand Jews for the entire war.

The Allies learned about the camps in early 1942, but they only weakly protested the murderous Nazi policies. It was not until 1944 that a War Refugee Board was established to rescue Jews and many State Department officials prevented escaped Jews from entering the United States. The Allies also rejected pleas to bomb the railroad facilities leading to the camps. They argued that diverting resources away from military targets would only prolong the war and hurt the chances of survival for the remaining Jews.

(above left) Thousands of wedding rings taken from death-camp inmates testify to the large number of Holocaust victims. (above right) Human bones are still visible in these concentration camp ovens where the corpses of executed Jews were burned. (below) These concentration camp survivors present a shocking testimony to Nazi atrocities during World War II.

pushed into Austria and Czechoslovakia. Fighting in Italy had ended, and the Americans were racing through Germany unopposed.

There was, however, a moment of sadness felt by the American troops amidst their triumph. On the night of April 12, 1945, President Roosevelt died of a massive cerebral hemorrhage at his retreat in Warm Springs, Georgia. In public appearances earlier in the year, the president had looked particularly worn and tired from his many travels. The years of pressure had finally taken their toll. Millions of Americans had grown up knowing only one president—FDR. He had been such a familiar part of their lives that soldiers in Europe and civilians at home wept openly when they heard the news. One soldier expressed a common emotion: "I felt as if I knew him. I felt as if he knew me—I felt as if he liked me." A special train took the president's body back to Washington. Thousands of Americans gathered along the railroad tracks to say goodbye.

The Nazis' Hidden Horrors

As they drove through Germany, the American soldiers discovered the hidden horrors of the Nazi regime. In April, the Americans liberated prisoners trapped in the horrifying concentration camps at Belsen, Buchenwald, and Dachau. In his attempt to establish a "pure" German race of light-skinned, blond-haired people, Hitler sent to the death camps those people who did not fit his ideal image. The Jews were one of Hitler's main targets for extermination. The Nazis had organized the systematic mass murder of all the Jews in Europe, and six million of them were killed in what became known as the Holocaust.

The camp survivors were little more than skin and bones. They had elongated limbs, shaven heads, and sunken eyes. They had barely enough energy to walk or eat. Corpses of prisoners were stacked on the open ground. The camp ovens were still filled with charred bones. The Americans found SS warehouses full of gold, valuables, and even hair that had been taken from the inmates. The stench of death was everywhere.

It was a sight no American GI could ever forget. They were ashamed to witness the unspeakable acts that their fellow human beings were capable of committing. Many soldiers were so disgusted by the grim scene that they immediately executed the SS troops that they found in the camps. American troops at Dachau forced German civilians from a nearby town, who claimed ignorance of the camp, to march past a pile of corpses. Schoolchildren, old men, and women marched by with lowered eyes. Eisenhower angrily insisted: "I want every American unit not actually in the front lines to see this place. Now at least, he will know what he is fighting against."

By the third week of April, the American Ninth Army was approaching the Elbe River, with Berlin less than one hundred miles away. Eisenhower faced a sensitive strategic dilemma: should he give the driving Americans the order to make a bold thrust to Berlin ahead of the Soviets? Eisenhower needed to balance political and military considerations. Roosevelt, Churchill, and Stalin had agreed to divide Germany into zones of occupation after the war was over. Berlin lay deep inside the Soviet zone, more than one hundred miles east of the proposed boundary of the British-American occupation zone. Even if the Americans captured Berlin, under the terms of the agreement, they would have to surrender all the territory they gained and pull back to their own zone.

There was some concern that an American assault might also provoke a clash with the Soviets, which the Americans did not

(above) As stunned Allied troops look on, a woman searches for the bodies of her relatives killed in Nazi camps. She covers her face in horror as well as to keep out the stench of death. (bottom left) A concentration camp survivor demonstrates for General Eisenhower some of the tortures the prisoners endured at Nazi hands. (bottom right) British prime minister Winston Churchill, U.S. president Harry Truman, and Soviet premier Joseph Stalin (from left to right) pose for the press at their meeting in Yalta.

(left) Forced by the war to abandon their home, a young German boy and his mother struggle to tow a cart loaded with their possessions. (right) A German woman salvages a few meager possessions as she flees the war's destruction.

want to risk. They anxiously needed the Soviets to honor their Yalta pledge to fight against Japan in Manchuria once the European war was finished. Eisenhower also feared an American attack would mean the sacrifice of more American lives. His staff estimated that they might suffer as many as 200,000 casualties in a fight for the city. Although the Americans could probably have driven to Berlin, Eisenhower decided the best course was to halt the American army's advance at the Elbe River. Above all, Eisenhower felt that the lives of his soldiers were worth more than the momentary prestige of capturing the city.

The Taste of Victory

On April 25, a tiny American patrol spotted units of the Red Army along the Elbe River near Torgau. The American soldiers jumped into boats and sped across to the other side. The GIs and Red Army troops shook hands and embraced, many with tears of joy in their eyes. They swore they would never forget the moment as long as they lived. The Americans gave the Soviets cigarettes and chewing gum, while the Soviets brought vodka and toasted the Americans. As Soviet soldiers played songs on an accordion, the two groups danced jubilantly. Photos show the soldiers grinning from ear to ear, with their arms wrapped around each other's shoulders. The issue of *Stars and Stripes* that commemorated the event sold more than one million copies. Its headline blared: "Yanks Meet Reds."

The final Soviet assault on Berlin had taken place two weeks before the meeting on the Elbe. Two separate Red Army forces, totaling three million men, approached the capital. Within ten days, they had completely encircled the city. The street fighting was exceptionally brutal. Fanatic SS units and Hitler Youth groups made diehard stands in apartment complexes, sewers, parks, and in the Berlin Zoo. Whole neighborhoods vanished under the Soviet artillery bombardment. The parliament building became a symbol of the last-ditch resistance of the Nazis. Five thousand SS troops barricaded themselves inside and fought room by room, story by story. After two days, the Soviets wiped out the last defenders, and two Red Army soldiers climbed to the roof of the building, where they placed the Soviet flag.

On April 28, Hitler was informed that the city's defenders had only enough ammunition to last for two more days. He spent most of the day composing his will. In the early hours of April 29, he married his mistress, Eva Braun, in a brief ceremony. The next day, he bid farewell to Goebbels and the other Nazi officials who stayed behind in the bunker. Then, Hitler and Braun returned to his private quarters. Moments later, a single shot was fired. Hitler and Braun had swallowed cyanide tablets together, and Hitler had also shot himself in the head. Their bodies were taken outside and burned. Two days later, negotiations between Allied and German generals over surrender terms began. On May 7, 1945, Gen. Alfred Jodl signed the unconditional surrender at Eisenhower's headquarters.

Churchill and Harry Truman, the new American president, declared May 8 as Victory in Europe Day (V-E Day). The streets of all the cities and towns across the United States were filled with crowds in wild celebration. Complete strangers kissed and hugged each other. People danced and sang in the streets. Ticker tape rained down from New York skyscrapers. V-E Day marked the end of the war in Europe, but soldiers were still fighting the war in the Pacific. The atomic bombing of Hiroshima on August 6, 1945, and of Nagasaki three days later resulted in the surrender of Japan. V-J Day, Victory over Japan Day, came on August 14.

The War's Aftermath

After the war, Europe lay in ruins. Its cities, factories, bridges, and farms had been destroyed. The amount of human suffering was also staggering. During the war, 50 million people died, and another 28 million were left homeless. By far the largest losses were borne by the Soviet Union, which had 20 million soldiers and civilians die. Nazi Germany lost 4 million men in battle and another 2 million civilians. The American battlefield deaths totaled 292,000, but the country escaped direct civilian casualties.

Taking into account this death and destruction, the ultimate question to be raised about the war is whether it was worth fighting. Given the staggering human cost, did defeating the Nazis justify the losses? It is tragic that often freedom and human dignity can be gained only by paying a high price. The loss of

(top) President Harry Truman greets victorious Allied commander Dwight Eisenhower at a postwar press conference at the White House. (bottom) The atomic bomb's effects on Hiroshima were immediate and terrible. Here, the bombed-out dome of the movie house stands amid the rubble.

(top left) Jubilant U.S. airmen, returning from Europe after the war, crowd an opening in their vehicle to get their first glimpse of home. (top right) The characteristic mushroom cloud of an atomic explosion rises above the Japanese city of Nagasaki on August 9, 1945. Japan surrendered five days later. (below) A German prisoner of war awaits processing at an Allied prison camp. The tag tells prison officials that he has an injured back.

life during World War II was appalling, but the Nazis had to be eliminated at almost any price. Everything Hitler stood for and everything he created was a threat to democracy, human decency, and fairness. His regime had to be overthrown.

After the war, there was also the question of who would pay for the suffering and hardships caused by the conflict. Should only the most guilty Nazis be punished, or should the entire German people somehow be forced to accept responsibility? The Allies prosecuted the most prominent Nazi leaders at war trials in Nuremberg. Nineteen Nazis were convicted of war crimes, and eleven were hanged. Other Nazis were tried by courts in the country where they committed their crimes.

The Denazification of Germany

The Allies also formally endorsed a policy for the denazification of Germany. People who had participated in the Nazi government or private citizens who had collaborated with the government were to be removed from their posts. At its high point, the Nazi party had eight million members. The business, academic, and government leaders of Germany were all Nazis, but the Americans and British only weakly enforced the denazification decree. Germany was faced with other, more serious problems. Its economy was in total chaos, its borders were overflowing with millions of incoming refugees, millions were homeless, and famine was becoming a pressing concern. The Allies felt the only way the country could be rebuilt was by using the skills and talents of the former Nazi leaders. Only 170,000 people were tried

The Nuremberg Trials

The idea that wars have rules that must be observed has been a principle of Western culture for centuries. The Nazis' mass murder of six million Jews was seen by the world as a violation of these rules. The Allied leaders warned the German leaders on numerous occasions during World War II that they would bring all war criminals to justice once the war was ended.

The trials of the leading Nazi officials began in Nuremberg, Germany, in November 1945 and lasted until August 1946. There were twenty-one defendants, taken from the German military command, the Nazi party, the government, the SS, and the gestapo, or secret police. Among the defendants were Hermann Göring, Albert Speer, Gen. Wilhelm Keitel, Gen. Alfred Jodl, the foreign minister Joachim von Ribbentrop, and governors of the occupied territories. Two more were indicted but never stood trial: Martin Boorman, who eluded capture, was a high-ranking Nazi party official and one of Hitler's closest advisors; and Gustav Krupp, the arms magnate who was declared too sick to stand trial. Goebbels and Himmler committed suicide before the war ended.

The prosecutors and judges were selected from the four major victorious powers: the United States, Great Britain, the Soviet Union, and France. The defendants were charged with war crimes against the peace (for launching the war) and war crimes against humanity (for their murderous policies toward the Jews and other civilians). They were allowed to have their own lawyers, and the trials were conducted by accepted legal rules and procedures. The evidence provided details of the horrors of the concentration camps, the mass execution of prisoners of war, and the torture and execution of civilians throughout Europe. None of the Nazis apologized for their actions. More often than not, their sole defense was: "I was only following orders."

Two of the defendants were acquitted. Speer and seven others received prison terms ranging from twenty years to life imprisonment. Ten went to the gallows in Nuremberg on October 16, 1946. Göring committed suicide by taking a cyanide pill the night before. The German bodies were cremated in the ovens of the Dachau concentration camp.

Some historians have argued that despite following proper legal procedures, the Nuremberg trials were unfair and were simply a way to punish the losers of the war. But the people in Europe who lived under Hitler's reign of terror regard the trials and the verdicts as just.

(left to right) Nazi leaders Hermann Göring, Rudolf Hess, Joachim von Ribbentrop, and Wilhelm Keitel sit in the front row at the Nuremberg court while they are tried for war crimes.

Many glorious European cities suffered great damage in the destruction of World War II, as these pictures of Nijmegen, Holland (above) and Munich, Germany (below right) show. (below left) The Nazi flag hangs over Wachenfeld House, Hitler's private country retreat in Obersalzberg.

for their wartime activities, and most received only minor punishments. Even the most notorious Nazis, with the right connections and a little luck, were able to obtain an entry visa to a foreign country. They were often aided in their escape by the American government, which appreciated their anticommunist beliefs. Numerous Nazi war criminals were discovered living in the United States after the war.

The entire geography of Europe was reshaped by World War II. As the war drew to a close, the continent's future was avidly discussed by world leaders. In a series of meetings at Tehran in Iran, Yalta in the Soviet Union, and Potsdam in Germany, Stalin, Churchill, Roosevelt, and later Truman hammered out the details of the new order in Europe. The Allied policy for the eastern part of Europe was particularly controversial. At war's end, the Red Army occupied all of eastern Europe with the exception of Greece, Albania, and Yugoslavia. The Soviet Union placed pro-Soviet leaders in position in Hungary, Czechoslovakia, Romania, Poland, and Bulgaria. The Soviets also annexed the Baltic states of Lithuania, Latvia, and Estonia. At the Yalta conference, Stalin promised the Allies that he would allow free elections in these countries, but he did not keep his word. Many criticized Roosevelt and Churchill for being naive and too trusting of Stalin, but in reality there was little they could do. The Soviet Union had twice been invaded by Germany within a single generation and it was the Soviet citizens who bore the heaviest losses in defeating the Nazis. Stalin was determined to ensure his nation's security. He wanted a buffer zone of friendly countries between the Soviet Union and the West.

The Allies decided that Germany would be divided along the Elbe River. The United States, Great Britain, and France had jurisdiction in the western half, and the Soviet Union had control of

Post-War Europe

the eastern half. Berlin, which was stranded inside the Soviet zone, was itself split into four sectors among the four powers. The Soviets guaranteed air and rail travel from Western-controlled Berlin into western Germany. The division of Germany was only intended as a temporary measure, but it lasted for more than forty years. West Germany formed a democratic government allied to the Americans and the Western countries. East Germany had a communist government imposed by Stalin. The construction of the Berlin Wall in 1961 symbolized the division of the nation.

With these postwar developments, an "iron curtain," in Churchill's famous phrase, descended upon Europe, dividing the continent into opposing halves. Europe west of the Elbe River was composed of capitalist democracies. East of the Elbe, communist political and economic systems were established that mirrored and were dominated by the Soviet Union. The Western European countries, along with the United States and Canada, formed a military alliance known as the North Atlantic Treaty

U.S. senator Joseph McCarthy reports on suspected communist activity in the United States at a congressional committee hearing in 1954. McCarthy's fanatic anticommunism led to a virtual witch-hunt.

Organization (NATO). The Soviet Union and the Eastern European states joined together in the Warsaw Pact. To help rebuild the devastated Western European economies, the United States, through the Marshall Plan, provided massive financial assistance and supplies. In the postwar decade, Europe received nearly fourteen billion dollars in U.S. aid and loans. Stalin refused to participate in the Marshall Plan, and as a result, Eastern Europe significantly lagged behind Western Europe in terms of economic development. The division of Europe lasted more than four decades. It was not until 1989, forty-four years after the war, that a wave of protests for democracy brought the downfall of the Berlin Wall, the reunification of Germany, and an end to communist rule in most of Eastern Europe.

The ideological division between the Eastern and Western blocs of Europe formed the basis of a political rivalry that dominated postwar international politics. The struggle between the United States and its allies and the Soviet Union became known as the Cold War. The Cold War produced great changes in U.S. domestic and foreign policies. For a time in the United States, members of communist and left-wing political organizations and their supporters were forbidden to hold positions as public servants, professors, teachers, and elected officials. This time of persecution in the 1950s was the result of the efforts of the prominent anticommunist Senator Joseph McCarthy to save the United States from the threat of communism. This unhealthy atmosphere of fear and suspicion affected American political and social life for a decade. In terms of international politics, the Cold War meant that the American government actively supported anticommunists, even to the extent of overthrowing democratically elected governments for fear that they were somehow sympathetic to communism. The long and costly involvement in Vietnam in the 1950s and 1960s was a direct result of the Cold War.

To help promote a "lasting peace" among nations around the world, the Allies agreed to the establishment of the United Nations after the war. The United Nations, as a successor to the defunct League of Nations, would develop and maintain friendly relations among nations and provide a multinational peacekeeping force to check military aggression. It would also coordinate international cooperation in solving economic problems of the poorer countries in the world. Despite the best intentions of the founders of the United Nations, wars are still being fought.

While most nations emerged from the war in worse shape than before, with their economies devastated and millions dead or wounded, the United States emerged from the war stronger than it had ever been. It became the world's strongest superpower, both militarily and economically.

The postwar economic boom created a period of unparalleled prosperity for Americans. Returning veterans and civilian workers across the country were eager to buy new houses, new cars, modern appliances, and other consumer goods. Increased consumption, the spread of suburbs and home ownership, and the rise of an affluent middle class can all be traced to the effects of war. Americans were optimistic about the future. A young woman named Laura Briggs recalled her feelings, "When the war was over, we felt really good about ourselves. We had saved the world from an evil that was unspeakable. Good times were going to go on and on; everything was going to get better. It was just a wonderful happy ending."

For Further Reading

Ronald Bailey, *Homefront USA*. Alexandria, VA: Time-Life Books Inc., 1977.

Nicholas Bethell, *Russia Besieged*. Alexandria, VA: Time-Life Books Inc., 1977.

Jonathan Croall, *Don't You Know There's A War On? The People's Voice*. London: Hutchins Radius, 1988.

Russell Freedman, *Franklin Roosevelt*. New York: Clarion Books, 1990.

Mark Harris et al., *The Homefront: America During WWII*. New York: Putnam, 1984.

Max Hastings, *Victory in Europe: D-Day—V-E Day*. Boston: Little, Brown & Co. Inc., 1985.

Leonard Mosely, *The Battle of Britain*. Alexandria, VA: Time-Life Books Inc., 1977.

David Nichols, ed., *Ernie's War: The Best of Ernie Pyle's WWII Dispatches*. New York: Random House Inc., 1986.

Cornelius Ryan, *A Bridge Too Far*. New York: Simon & Schuster, 1974.

Cornelius Ryan, *The Longest Day*. New York: Simon & Schuster, 1959.

A.J.P. Taylor, *The Second World War: An Illustrated History*. New York: G.P. Putnam's Sons, 1975.

Robert Wallis, *The Italian Campaign*. Alexandria, VA: Time-Life Books Inc., 1978.

Douglas Cameron Watt, *How War Came*. New York: Pantheon Books Inc., 1989.

Works Consulted

John Erickson, *The Road to Stalingrad*. New York: Harper & Row, 1975.

Edwin Hoyt, *The GI's War*. New York: McGraw-Hill Inc., 1988.

John Keegan, *The Second World War*. New York: Viking Penguin, 1989.

Chris McDonald, *The Battle of the Bulge*. London: Weidenfeld and Nicolson, 1984.

Studs Terkel, *The Good War: An Oral History of WWII*. New York: Pantheon Books Inc., 1984.

Index

Photo Credits

About the Author

John J. Vail is a graduate of the University of Chicago and holds a Ph.D. in political science from Rutgers University. He is the author of numerous books for young adults, including biographies of Fidel Castro, Nelson Mandela, and Thomas Paine. His books have been translated into seven languages and have been cited for excellence by the New York Public Library and *School Library Journal*.